THE DIVORCED DAD DILEMMA

*A Father's Guide to Understanding, Grieving and
Growing
Beyond the Losses of Divorce
And to Developing a Deeper, Ongoing Relationship
with His Children*

**By
Gerald S. Mayer, Ph.D.**

Authors Choice Press
San Jose New York Lincoln Shanghai

The Divorced Dad Dilemma
A Father's Guide to Understanding, Grieving and Growing
Beyond the Losses of Divorce And to Developing a Deeper,
Ongoing Relationship with His Children

Authors Choice Press
an imprint of iUniverse.com, Inc.

For information address:
iUniverse.com, Inc.
5220 S 16th, Ste. 200
Lincoln, NE 68512
www.iuniverse.com

Originally published by Desert City Press

ISBN: 0-595-14192-7

Printed in the United States of America

Nuber

For My Father;
I miss him still.

Acknowledgements

I owe a great debt to the men and women who sit across from me in my office and share their pain, their passions, and their triumphs. They are pseudonymously presented in this book, with identifying information carefully disguised. My humble vignettes in no way do justice to the richness and the texture of their lives.

Friends, colleagues, and mentors have offered invaluable support and encouragement, sometimes in ways they may not know. Bruce Jacobson put forward valuable suggestions on an earlier draft. More importantly, he has been a steadfast friend during the long silences that seem to characterize many men's relationships, including ours. Cathy Smith believed in this project and my ability to bring it to fruition before I did. She is a perceptive and empathetic friend and colleague. John Zell offered both caring and wisdom as I slowly developed the insight and perspective necessary to write this book.

Of course, those closest to me affect me most deeply. My mother is a source of both emotional support and astute clinical observation. My brother, Larry, unflagging in his encouragement, is a compassionate man and a good friend. Each of my children is remarkable in his or her own way. Jacob has reacquainted me with the simple joys and monumental challenges of boyhood. Heather is full of the warmth and uncorrupted creativity of childhood, even as she aspires to be a "big girl". Finally, so much of who I am today is an outgrowth of my relationship with Kate. My pen would never have touched paper without her.

CONTENTS

Introduction

Over the years, as I have moved with halting steps along the bumpy road of my own journey, it has become much less of a secret from myself why my work with fathers, struggling in their relationships with their children, strikes such a responsive emotional chord in me. As a therapist, I believe strongly that I could be of little value to such men, often deeply grieving and confused over the losses in their life following divorce, until I came to grips with my own losses and the impact they had on my life.

After decades of divorce being considered an acceptable relationship outcome, the tide of popular and, perhaps, professional opinion has moved toward avoiding divorce, as well as toward acknowledging the long shadow divorce can cast in the lives of children and adults. Indeed, much of my practice is devoted to helping couples move to a healthier, more intimate level of relatedness. Despite best intentions and efforts, however, divorces will continue to occur.

Divorce is usefully considered a crisis of transition, a crisis that can be understood in terms of individual and family disruption and reorganization. The developmental tendency that emerges from this crisis, painful and confusing as it may be, is to move forward to a new level of functioning which allows individuals and families (however they are constituted and defined) the best opportunity to grow and provide nurturance. It has been my observation that it is often men's response to relationship separation and to the disruption of their connection to their children that stymies this growth process.

The focus of this book is necessarily a biased one. My own life experience exerts its influence throughout. It is men's responses to the losses of divorce, their internal emotional struggle, their attempts to solve the dilemma of connectedness in their lives, that are the rightful subjects of this book. We must remember that whenever we magnify an aspect of a complicated dynamic, such as men's relationships with their children in the context of divorce, our sense of perspective becomes distorted. Yet, sometimes we must look closely to understand fully.

As a man, working to the best of my ability to understand myself and my relationship world, I have been struck by the simplistic, polarizing characterizations of men that pervade much of our culture. Such ideas, it seems to me, only serve to perpetuate the blaming and shaming that inflame the issue of gender differences and serve to obscure the opportunity for individual and social change. I have tried, perhaps not always successfully, to avoid such characterizations. In discussing men's emotional woundedness and the challenge of relatedness to children and others, I have labored also to honor the clearly positive virtues that men offer their loved ones. In discussing the role of women in men's lives and in men's woundedness, I have endeavored to avoid any suggestion of intentionality or blame in what is a very complicated, multifaceted issue. Furthermore, my writing is based primarily on my personal and professional experiences in the dominant culture. To the extent that different social mores and structures impact how we think, feel, and relate, my impressions may be generalized to different subcultures only with great caution.

Consider this book an invitation to a journey, a journey toward understanding self and increasing one's sense of relatedness to others. The structure of the book is quite simple. The first half of the book (Part I) is a "statement of the problem," focusing on the many factors impacting divorced men's relationships with their children. Chapter One examines loss as a normal and necessary aspect of the parenting experience. In Chapter Two, the broader issue of attachment and loss, especially as these phenomena relate to divorce and relationship separation, are discussed. Chapter Three speaks to the important area of men and grief. Some of the social and cultural factors that impact men's capacity to deal with powerful feelings, as well as the various mechanisms (some healthy, some not) that men may use to cope with their painful feelings, are spelled out. In Chapter Four, the nature of the losses associated with divorce are examined. Particular attention is paid to men's vulnerability to divorce, the ambivalent and ambiguous nature of the "divorce loss," and the difficulty of maintaining attachment to children. I also address the relationship perils of the "wounded" divorced man. Chapter Five deals more directly with the powerful past experiences that impact male emotionality, reactions to relationship separation and loss, and men's attempts to maintain meaningful relationship connections.

Part II is about learning to successfully grieve and grow

beyond separation and loss to a new level of self-acceptance and connectedness to our loved ones, particularly our children. In Chapter Six, I encourage the reader to take a "loss inventory" and clarify their past losses and other factors that may be impacting them currently. Dealing with shame and guilt, the twin demons of manhood, as well as developing an authentic male emotionality, is the topic of Chapter Seven. Chapter Eight focuses on knowing when we need help from others, finding it, and learning to ask for this help. The reality of maintaining relationships with our own children, during and following the divorce process, is underscored in Chapter Nine. Specific techniques and skills for staying connected with our children, despite complicated lives, are offered in this chapter. Chapter Ten tackles the often sensitive topic of coparenting with a former spouse. Finally, Chapter Eleven broaches the issue of new attachments-- a healthy, adult, love relationship, while dealing with our feelings and the complications associated with our continuing relationship with our children.

Fathers with full-time custody of their children, or fathers with no contact with their children, will find issues discussed in this book relevant to their situation. *However, this book is primarily intended for fathers who have significant contact with their children but encounter unexpected pain or impediments. This book is also for those men with little contact with their children who have found their own emotional issues to be a block to continuing some level of meaningful, consistent connection.* All these men may struggle daily with the difficult tasks of being a man and providing nurturance, of grieving well and letting go, of loving children and respecting the child they once were, of being strong and offering tenderness, of yearning for simplicity in a world of complications. These are men who, by virtue of this struggle, have an opportunity to enrich their own lives and the lives of their children. This book is for them.

PART I

Attachment and Loss:

The Divorced Dad Dilemma

*Life can be counted on
to provide all the pain
that any of us might
possibly need.*

-- Sheldon Kopp, *An End to Innocence*

One

Parenting and Loss

I realized at that moment that I was never going to come home again and see Annie at the top of the stairs; never going to see her again at our breakfast table in her nightgown and socks. I suddenly realized what was happening; Annie was all grown up and leaving us. And something inside began to hurt.

> --Steve Martin in *Father of the Bride*
> c *1991 Touchstone Pictures*

When all is said and done, even under the best of circumstances, parenting is about loss. Indeed, if we are honest with ourselves, despite all the many other rewards, raising children is fraught with loss. The transition from the breast or bottle to other foods, the capacity to respond to people other than Mom or Dad, crawling and the first, halting steps, gleefully running away and hiding, the first day at preschool--all these are occasions for joy and wonder at a child's growth and development. Yet, our joy is bittersweet, for mixed with our joy is curious sadness. This sadness, this grief, unless denied, follows us throughout our parenting years. We soon come to realize that every step forward our child takes is also a step away.

> *Chuck and Susan drove somewhat uneasily toward the school for their daughter, Sarah's, first day of school. As they entered the parking lot, Sarah squealed with excitement, while Susan's eyes welled up with tears. Chuck parked the car, and barely a second after it came to rest, Sarah bounded confidently out of the car door and toward the school. Chuck and Susan had just caught up with her when a smiling woman, Sarah's teacher, greeted her and invited her into the classroom. With only a quick hug and scarcely a backward glance, Sarah entered the classroom and, in so doing, moved one more step away from Mom and Dad and into a larger world of other adults and children. Chuck*

comforted a tearful Susan as they exited the school. A few minutes later, he dropped Susan off at work and proceeded towards his office. It was then, alone and in the safety of his car, that Chuck allowed himself to experience his feelings about his daughter's first day of school. He wasn't sure if he was sad or just a bit "out of sorts." Over the subsequent years, Chuck learned to identify that feeling as one which arose when his child passed a milestone in her life, when, in some small way, his world changed forever.

The future holds more joy...and more grief. So many of these milestones often wound us in ways we will not admit, even to ourselves, for they involve our own sense of self. These changes harken our gradual, but necessary demotion in the hearts and minds of our children from the status of gods to that of mere mortals. Our son comes to realize that we are not the biggest and strongest and smartest man in the world. Our daughter eagerly vies for the attention of some boy in her fifth grade class, perhaps much in the same way she once sought to see herself reflected in our eyes. Special songs and pet names are lost, too soon it seems, to the years. We would have it no other way, as we take justified pride in our children's healthy growth and separation. Yet, our intimately connected relationship with our children is so unlike any other involvement in our adult world that we may be forgiven some pause before we let go. But let go we must. And in our joy, in our pride, we must also acknowledge our pain.

Frank felt pleased that he had been given two tickets for that evening's baseball game. Going to baseball games had always been a special time for Frank and his son. Many a summer evening was spent at the ball park, rooting for their favorite team, eating hotdogs, and playing baseball trivia games. Needless to say, Frank was stunned when he made the offer to go to the game and his son turned him down.

"I'm going with my buddies. Sorry Dad," said the boy.

Frank good naturedly said, "Good," and offered the tickets he had purchased to his son. That night, Frank got out his old glove and ball. He smelled the old leather and replayed the days of playing catch with his son. He longed to play just one more inning of a make-believe World Series game. He tossed the ball into the air aimlessly a couple of times. Then he shrugged his shoulders and put the ball and glove away in the closet. He felt alone. After seasons of faithful play, Frank was no longer a starter. His son had relegated him to the bench.

Adolescence, by its very nature, is a time for our children to pull away and "test their wings." The wild swings between an assertive, sometimes aggressive, independent stance, and the visits home for food, money, a warm bed, and a kind word, are reminders of the days of the young child defiantly running away from Mom, but then returning for emotional refueling. If, as parents, we are unaware of this process, we run the risk of prematurely pushing our child away or regressively holding on, with both these maneuvers in service of avoiding our own pain at continuous arrivals and leave-takings. Many a parent has insisted a child leave home at some arbitrary age or stage, not out of any coherent belief about the appropriateness of such a move, but more out of a desire to come to some sense of closure, out of a wish to heal their own wounding by an adolescent child's successive attempts to separate.

Bill, a successful construction contractor, at age 35 found himself becoming increasingly irritated and angry as his youngest son, Ron, reached his 17th birthday. Ron, bright, conscientious, and ambitious, would soon be graduating from high school, a full year ahead of his peers. Despite good grades, he found himself unsure of whether he wanted to immediately continue his studies at a local college. Instead, he considered working for a year before attending school. As graduation approached and Ron's plans remained uncrystallized, Bill began to angrily repeat that if Ron did not go to school, he would be out on his own, working full-time and supporting himself. "When I was 17, I was working, married, and had one child, with another on the way," he bellowed. Not surprisingly, Ron, on angry impulse, moved away from home the afternoon of the last day of school. He didn't even

*attend his graduation ceremony. Bill claimed that he
was relieved to have both of his sons out of the house.
"Now my wife and I can begin to enjoy life," was Bill's
standard line for public consumption. But in moments
of quiet reflection, when he was by himself, Bill found
his mind sadly wandering back to his own adolescent
"coming of age," a time that had come upon him too
suddenly and violently; and to his time with his own
children, time that had passed too quickly and ended
with too much hurt.*

Subsequent years bring more change, as children
grow up, move away from home, and move on with their
own lives, often entering their own marriages and raising
their own children. This, too, brings with it the curious, sad,
satisfaction that comes with a job done well enough to be
considered finished.

So it seems that our relationships with our children
must be intermittently revised and grieved as they more
along in their gradual and natural passage from infant
dependency to adult self-sufficiency. It is in light of this
awareness that we can begin to understand our strong emotional reactions when this process is accelerated or distorted,
if short absences become long separations, if routine "good-
nights" are divided by many days or weeks, if the comings
and goings of day-to-day family living are replaced by
painful leave-takings and awkward reunions. Often, these are
the circumstances of men's relationships with their children
following divorce. These are the circumstances that test the
bond between a father and his child, a bond that begins
before birth and lasts a lifetime.

What, then, is this powerful bond with our children?
Why is it so strong? Why do we hurt when it changes? Why
may we devastated emotionally by separation from our children? These questions have many answers, depending on our
personal histories and life experiences. For all of us, though,
the beginning point in finding the answers come with understanding the process of attachment.

Two

Attachments Made, Attachments Broken

I keep remembering how great I felt when I carried her for the first time. She was so small, so perfect. I think I was kind of in shock, maybe a little afraid of my own feelings.
But I knew then that my life would never be the same, and that was fine with me. I never thought of not being with her.
Now that I don't see her much, except every other month or so, it's like there's a piece of me missing, like I'm a little dead inside, you know what I mean?

*--*25 year old Nick, *six months after moving out of his home and three months after his ex-wife and daughter moved to another state.*

The loss of important relationships, changes in the nature of relationships to others, changes in our emotional and physical selves, are a necessary part of normal development. The father may feel "outside" the close physical and emotional connection between mother and infant. The young child moves away from the sense of oneness with mother. Mother and father gradually "let go" of the developing child. The adolescent revises the relationships with his or her parents. The incremental failure of our bodies as we age, the loss of peers to death, and, finally, our own mortality, are a few of the normal losses we encounter. Our capacity for grief upon experiencing a loss assumes a strong connection, or a cognitive and emotional "taking in" of our parents, our siblings, our friends, our spouses, and our children.

Attachment and Loss

The experience of grief is not just a function of loss, but a function of the nature of the attachment of the individual to the lost relationship. It is clear that attachment behavior is a normal life-long process that has its basis in childhood. Just as our need to develop and maintain attachments continues throughout our lives, so does our vulnerability to separation and loss Our early relationships with our parents, particularly how the issues of "closeness and distance" were managed in the relationship, has ongoing implications for our later ability to tolerate closeness and separation in subsequent relationships. Finally, it is the reciprocal relationships between individuals in a family unit that offer a context for the attachment dynamic to unfold.

Members of a family engage in complementary activities of communication and caregiving, allowing each individual to develop an internal representation of him or herself in interaction with others.   These current relationships resonate with each individual's experiences with past relationships.   Thus, the normal human strivings to bond and "take in" connections with others as part of ongoing family relationships accounts for our sense of attachment to others. It is in this developing matrix of attachment phenomena, played out in our heads and hearts and between ourselves and our loved ones, that the warmth, the calm, the solace, and the joy of secure relationships occurs So, too, is it from the disruption of these attachments that our anxiety, pain, and grief flows forth.

> *Joe, a hard-working computer technician, considered himself very much a "family man." When not working, Joe could almost always be found at his home, either tinkering at various odd jobs or watching sports on television. While not a particularly emotional man, Joe took particular pride and comfort in the fact that his family situation was much different than the chaotic situation that existed in the alcoholic family in which he was raised. He experienced his marriage as solid and predictable. For Joe, family life was warm and nurturing in the sense of supplying a supportive emotional network for him.*

> *After some 15 years of marriage, Joe's wife returned to school to pursue a degree in sociology and, shortly thereafter, confronted Joe with her long-term unhappiness in the marriage. She stated her desire to terminate the relationship as a marriage but communicated her continued affection and respect for Joe, as well as her wish to continue to coparent their three children with him. Joe received this news with some initial shock but*

*quickly reverted to the rational, controlled style he was
most comfortable with. However, in the ensuing days
and weeks, as their marital separation and impending
divorce became more real to Joe, he found himself
increasingly anxious, sad, and unable to concentrate.
On many a night, he found himself lying awake, listening to his heart beating rapidly, with a sense of panic
and impending doom that he dimly recalled from an
earlier time and place.*

How We Grieve

Bowlby (1982) presents a predictable sequence of grief-
related behaviors which occur in young children when bonding
with the primary parent or caretaker is disrupted. Specifically, he
outlines a three-phase model of: (1) *protest,* during which the
child reacts with anger and anguish in an attempt to signal pain
and bring about prompt reunion, (2) *despair,* when the reality sets
in that the reunion will not soon take place, and (3) *detachment,*
a mode of social withdrawal and defensive indifference which
often continues, even if the grieved relationship is restored.
While these phases are based on young children's reactions to
significant loss, we can recognize similar patterns in ourselves
and other adults when faced with traumatic relationship loss.
Several theorists, including Kubler-Ross (1969), Parks (1972),
and Wolfelt (1988), have developed stage models which seek to
explain the normal experience of grief in response to the death of
a loved one. These models tend to depict the mourner as moving
from a position of shock, numbness, and disbelief, to extreme
emotional upset, a sense of emptiness, and frequent bodily aches
and pains, then finally (often months or even years later) to
acceptance, as evidenced by a moving on with one's life. As
helpful as these models may be, it is very important to realize that
grieving is very much a personal experience, influenced by our
past experiences, our culture, and our unique emotional makeup.
Therefore, these outlines of the grief process are best considered
rough approximations, with much overlap between stages and
occasional repetition of previously experienced stages. In fact, a
common phenomenon that I have noticed in myself and those I
have worked with in clinical practice is a kind of "plateau" which
may last weeks, months, or even years, and then reemerge in

response to a similar loss, an anniversary or birthday, a marriage, the birth of a child, or some other important life cycle event.

The Divorce Process

Writers on the loss of divorce also emphasize a developmental process. Kessler (1975) has developed a six-stage paradigm: (1) *disillusionment*, the initial period of disenchantment and finding fault with the marriage; (2) *erosion*, a period of emotional divorce, when mutuality in a relationship falters; (3) *detachment*, when investment in the relationship ends and thoughts about the future and fantasies about being single or of other relationships predominate; (4) *separation*, in which actual physical separation occurs and stress tends to be at its highest level; (5) *mourning*, as feelings of anger, hurt, and sadness over the ''death of the marriage'' are worked through, and (6) *recovery*, when acceptance of the end of the marriage occurs, some degree of objectivity about the marriage and the former spouse develops, and new relationships and pursuits are emotionally invested in.

In my own experience, it is during these last three phases of separation, mourning, and recovery that many men falter, either by getting ''stuck'' in a position of emotional detachment, by remaining in a state of deep shame and guilt, or by precipitously plunging ahead into new attachments or activities, all in a misdirected attempt to assuage their pain. To understand this common problem we must first examine why we may have so much difficulty tolerating grief and doing the work of mourning. Second, we must appreciate the specific aspects of the divorce trauma that make moving beyond it so problematic for so many men.

<u>Three</u>

Big Boys Don't Cry: Men and Grief

*Control. I couldn't let go because I had to be in control of my
emotions. I had to be in control of my world, and, whenever possible
other people's worlds as well. ...I always had to be in control.
I could never be late. I couldn't stand to be kept waiting--
Control in a hundred different ways.
If I could just control or maintain the illusion of control by predicting
and programming my existence and environment,
I thought that I might just have a chance in this world.*

--John Lee in *The Flying Boy: Healing the Wounded Man*

In western society, the grief responses of women and men appear to differ. A woman's grief is more likely to be visible, directly expressed, and socially sanctioned. From birth on, men tend to be reinforced for suppressing their feelings, for "taking care of business" and for never complaining about their pain and discomfort. How often have we witnessed, either in our lives or on television or in the movies, the stereotyped scene of the grief-stricken, "overwrought" woman and the strong, silent, comforting man? Raised to fill a "hero" role in society, these "weekday warriors" find themselves rewarded for being out in the world, separated from home and family, and devoted to work and production. All too often, the time-honored functions of provider and protector become only caricatures of men's roles, without a capacity for intimate relatedness and authentic male emotionality to provide balance. It is little surprise that many of us find ourselves with neither the emotional skills nor the social support to cope with the pain of relationship separation and loss.

The Twin Demons: Shame and Guilt

In my work with so many men seeking to better understand their emotional life and trying to express their feelings productively, it has become very clear to me that many of us experience deep shame over our feelings and the sense of unfamiliar vulnerability that comes with them. This inner sense of being diminished or insufficient as a person is, I believe, often the central issue for men as they deal with loss We simply are not trained to cope with losses that cannot be undone, nor with problems that do not lend themselves to quick solutions. We may express shame over the loss itself, believing that it would never have occurred if we were truly adequate or in control. Shame may occur as a pervasive state in response to the emergence of sadness, confusion, anger, and the accompanying sense of vulnerability. Equating independence with maturity and worthiness, shame over our sense of aloneness and our impotence to change this sense of isolation may become extreme. As we shall see later, the issue of men's shame is particularly important and complicated in the case of divorce.

Many men report episodes of powerful rage in reaction to loss. In my own work with men, I have been struck with the interwoven nature of men's rage and their underlying shame and fear. Ashamed and fearful over their vulnerability and impotence in the face of loss, many of us may react with defensive rage. This mechanism is very ineffective, of course, because while it may restore a temporary sense of control and power, it ultimately results in increased shame and social isolation. Indeed, as part of my work with men who experience frequent or disruptive episodes of destructive rage, I often teach them to ask themselves the simple questions, "What am I ashamed of?" and "What am I afraid of?" This may allow some men to more accurately identify their underlying feelings and to begin to change their responses. By the same token, many of us may need help in feeling entitled to our normal anger and its healthy expression before it becomes bottled up, imbued with shame, and explosive.

Other men demonstrate another classic shame response, that of silence, in response to loss. Grief may be felt, but it is not expressed or fully processed. Moments of deep sadness may be pushed away in the presence of others. Attempts to engage the mourner in discussion may be met by efforts to avert his gaze, change the subject, or actually physically distance himself. While the "silent mourner" may, in some instances, engage in a more or less full grieving process, he may still have deep shame over his internal experience and find himself cut off from others.

While perhaps not as toxic emotionally as deep shame, many men's focus on performance and achievement may result in a painful residue of enormous guilt over relationships separation or divorce. Guilt, as opposed to shame, is a response to not *behaving* in a manner that meets an internal standard. (Shame, as previously discussed, is a deeper, less boundaried experience that relates to the *self* as unworthy or defective.) While relationship separation, divorce, or death are complicated phenomena often lying partially or completely outside an individual's range of influence, some men still accept inordinate responsibility for relationship outcomes.

Thus, guilt can be a healthy response when it moves us toward a reasonable standard of behavior in an area where we have both a degree of responsibility and influence. Unhealthy guilt is based on an assumption of responsibility, influence, and the possibility of repair, when these conditions do not exist. Clearly, remaining stuck in a guilt-driven attempt to change what we cannot change is an impediment to engaging in the process of healthy and necessary grieving and moving on with one's life.

Overworking and other Pain-Avoidance Strategies

Socialized to see life as a problem to be solved, rather than a process to be experienced, some men throw themselves into a pattern of compulsive ''doing'', often centered on work. In our culture, work is a major source of identity for men. Under the stress of loss, whether the loss involves a relationship, financial status, aging, or physical change related to illness or an accident, many of us may attempt to balm our woundedness with hours of unnecessary work. Indeed, in the midst of emotional pain and change, some men may see their relationship with work and productiyity as the *one* relationship which has not been ruptured or damaged.

> *Phil was born into a large family in the mid-West. His father was a hardworking man who spent most of his time away from the family home. Phil's mother was described as a controlling, emotionally ungiving woman. Indeed, in Phil's family, there was little emotional expression, little talk about individual wants or*

needs, and much focus on what one was doing rather than what one was feeling. Phil found out quite early that success in school was one way to receive praise and attention. Indeed, academic achievement became the way that he managed his sense of worth and self-esteem. When Phil left for college, he had little sense of who he really was, little connection with his feelings, and no real capacity to experience himself as separate from the rigid rules and expectations of the family he came from. Later in his college career, Phil married a woman who required much attention and emotional nurturing from him.

After graduating from college, Phil got a job with a large corporation and set out to live what he perceived at that point to be "the American dream." In his heart, Phil believed that with hard work and perseverance, as well as loyalty to the corporation, that he would be able to achieve a top position in the firm. As the years went on, Phil was asked to make various geographic moves, each one causing significant disruption in his marital and family life, and each one requiring Phil to make adjustments to new social and work situations. In each setting, Phil worked harder, lost previous social connections and friendships, pulled further and further away from his wife and family, and became increasingly isolated from his feelings.

Not surprisingly, Phil's wife left him, citing his overinvolvement in work and his inability to meet her emotional needs. Phil believed that his wife would eventually return to him, so he responded to this stress by involving himself further in work. Shortly thereafter, Phil's corporation underwent a major reorganization. He was given a choice to either leave the company or accept a position for which he was not truly suited, at a much lower rate of pay. Phil became quite depressed, indecisive, and unable to cope with this decision. After years of focusing his intellectual and emotional energy on his work life, and neglecting his relationship, family life, and other pursuits, Phil found himself feeling lost, empty, and confused.

Other attempts to immerse ourselves in activity to avoid

pain may center on exercise, chores around the house, or successful sexual encounters. Some men speak of their sexual activities
in terms of "conquest" or as a way to express anger at women,
or as a way to shore up damaged self-esteem by confirming their
attractiveness or continued desirability. Some men simply seek
a kind of addictive "high." For others, however, the issue that
emerges over time is the wish to be close, to be warm, to be held,
to make contact, without taking the risk of true emotional intimacy.

Using alcohol or other drugs is a common way of
deadening feelings, weakening inhibitions, and lubricating social
interaction. But the risk for developing an addictive relationship
to a drug is quite high, especially for those men with a family
history of alcoholism or other drug addiction, or a personal history
of chemical-related problems. Chemical addiction may start
slowly, then grow into the dominant feature of an individual's life.
We also know that, in addition to alcohol and other drugs, a
number of behaviors or processes can take on compulsive or
addictive proportions, including work, various types of sexual
behavior, or exercise. Whenever an addictive process exists, this
primary disease must be arrested before underlying issues can be
addressed successfully.

<u>Buying a Porsche: Defense or Addiction?</u>

There is a difference between an entrenched addiction
and a temporary behavioral strategy used to avoid extreme pain.
Defenses, whether psychological or behavioral, exist for a reason. Not everyone confronts pain in the same way. Under some
circumstances, such as a sudden and severe relationship loss,
throwing oneself into work, buying a new red Porsche, exercising
daily, or jamming one's calendar with multiple social engage-
ments may be a temporary, but necessary, mechanism to dull
immediate emotional anguish. Initially, such behaviors may be
essential for men who may well find themselves without the
emotional skills or the social networking so important in process-
ing loss. As a therapist, I have found that what is most helpful to
a man early in the grief process is to identify ways of coping that
appear to be least harmful and to have the least addictive
potential. What I have found to be most destructive is a sudden

attempt to prematurely strip the griever of his defensive mechanisms This tends to be what men fear most strongly and may be
the surest way to scare a man, already feeling vulnerable and out
of control, away from a tenuous commitment to understanding
his emotional life and experiencing his feelings

Growing from Addiction to Grief

Meaningful growth always involves the gradual development of new coping methods and more flexible defenses. as
well as the release of old, less effective mechanisms As these old
strategies for avoiding pain are replaced by more flexible mechanisms that allow us to experience and process grief, underlying
issues can then emerge In my years of working with men in the
first year or two of recovery from addiction. I have found that it
is the rule, rather than the exception, that deep, unprocessed grief
over childhood or later loss emerges

> *Rick sat in my office and wept Two years after his last*
> *drink of alcohol. one year into his recovery from com-*
> *pulsive sexual behavior, after a failed marriage and*
> *several unsuccessful other attempts at relationships*
> *with women. Rick's sadness centered on two major*
> *losses a childhood in which he was not protected,*
> *respected, and cherished; and his relationship with his*
> *now adult daughter who had begun to evidence the*
> *same pattern of painful relationships and overuse of*
> *chemicals that had characterized her father's life.*
> *Though nothing needed to be said to Rick at that point.*
> *his commitment to working on himself had borne the*
> *fruit of deep grieving. grieving no longer buried and*
> *"stuck" in time by his own addictive and compulsive*
> *behavior.*

What is clear is that for many men, perhaps for most men,
initiating and proceeding through the tasks of mourning is both
painful and unfamiliar, even under the best of circumstances
Unfortunately, the loss attendant to divorce is not the best of
circumstances By its very nature, divorce is sown with emotional landmines that may not only injure, but leave us frustrated
and confused, and, all too often, regressively pulled back to an old
relationship or prematurely propelled forward to a new one

Four

Living With An Open Wound:
The Special Nature of the Divorce Loss

As soon as I finally get used to being without them, it's time to go see them again. I walk up to the door of what used to be my house, full of this mixture of anxiety and joy. I'm always happy to see the kids. Sometimes it's even good to see their Mom. It's not usually comfortable at first, I think because I know it's not going to last. When it's time to say goodbye, that's when it hurts. The kids don't understand why Dad has to go, and really, I don't understand all the time, either. For hours, after I drop them off, I feel really down. Then, when I stop missing them, I start to feel really guilty. The whole thing is pretty crazy. I sometimes wonder if this is even worth it.

    -- 32 year old Hector, divorced for 6 months, *commenting on the difficult arrivals and leavetakings of the shared custody of his seven year old son and five year old daughter.*

    The list of potential losses usually associated with divorce is devestating. There is the loss of the adult sexual relationship, with its loss of hopes and dreams for the future. There are the losses of financial resources and mutual friends and activities. There is the powerful loss of the structure, order, permanence, and predictability of the intact family, and the sense of "home". Further, there is the loss of extended family and of family ritual. Finally, there is loss of children (at the very least, the type of relationship one had with children prior to the divorce). Some men often underestimate the collective magnitude of these multiple losses, defensively focusing on more tangible aspects of the divorce, such as the loss of home or a portion of income. Yet, virtually every father I have worked with that has considered a divorce has voiced a clear fear about losing his relationship with his children. (Indeed, even before a divorce, unhappily married men report a fear of losing their children as a paramount reason for staying in a troubled union.) As time progresses, the toll of the less quantifiable aspects of the divorce is felt. Fathers who are separated from their home and children undergo a change in self-concept and, almost certainly, a lowering of self-esteem. We may feel emotionally uprooted without familiar structure and relationships. At times like this, we may even feel as if we no longer know who we are. We have lost a central element of our male identity.

> *When I first met Gary, a successful salesman, he was in a very unhappy, 10 year old marriage. Gary and his wife, Christy, had married early in college after Christy became pregnant with their first child. At that time, Gary (whose own natural father left his mother when he was not yet two years old) was determined to be a good father and husband. Yet, despite the best of intentions, considerable commitment, attempts at individual and couples therapy, and a mutual devotion to their two children, Gary and Christy were unable to resolve their serious differences. Although he was quite uncomfortable with the idea, Gary began to talk seriously about the prospect of separating. Then, one day, Gary informed me that he had decided to discontinue therapy, saying he would not leave his family and that he would just "grind it out." I did not hear from Gary again for about three months. At that time, I received an urgent call from him requesting an emergency appointment. When I saw him, Gary looked tired and worn. His voice trembled when he spoke. "I left last week," he said. "I've moved into a studio apartment. And it's been terrible. I can't sleep. My appetite is gone. I can't concentrate at work. It's like I've lost my confidence. I don't even want to try selling. And I miss my kids. It just wasn't supposed to be this way."*

Men's Vulnerability

While it serves no meaningful purpose to engage in the debate over whether men or women are more negatively impacted by divorce, it is interesting to note that there is some evidence that men may be at greater risk for emotional disturbance, especially at the time of, and just following, the separation. Popular stereotypes to the contrary, wives are much more likely to initiate a divorce than are their husbands. The person who initiates the divorce, usually the woman, has often had some opportunity to work through the divorce process for some time prior to action being taken. The consequent "abandoned male syndrome" (Myers, 1986) may show itself as extreme anger, denial, suppression of other feelings, and a defensive flight into activity. Disavowing their own dependency needs, while adopting a familiar, strong, silent, "hero" role, some men have long gotten their emotional and social affiliation needs met through their relationship with a woman. When the relationship ends, especially when it is abruptly interrupted, these men are "caught short." Their self-image undergoes amputation.

Ambivalence and Grief

Divorce, by its very nature, is an unclear ending to a highly ambivalent relationship. Every relationship is characterized by some measure of ambivalence. It is when we lose a relationship that is highly ambivalent, where strong feelings of love coexist with strong disappointment, hurt, and anger, that our grieving is most likely to be difficult and complicated. It is a paradox that the more positive and beneficial the relationship, the greater may be our capacity to cope with its loss. While losing such a relationship is very upsetting, the loss may be characterized by manageable disappointment and frustration, and grieved in a way that allows for some emotional closure.

While extremely traumatic in other ways, at least the death of a loved one has some potential for a clearer ending. This is, I believe, one of the reasons that unhappy spouses, at the expense of extreme guilt, may fantasize about the death of their partner. When someone dies, we may see them dead. We may witness them being placed in a coffin; and we may attend their funeral. With divorce, we have to deal with the death of a hope, a dream, a type of relationship, and a lifestyle, while the person we were married to is still very much alive and, in many cases, a continuing part of our lives. *This is especially so if we share children with her.* Grieving the loss of a dream, a relationship, and a family unit, while we still experience a certain level of real emotional investment in a frequently present person, makes the tasks of mourning enormously difficult.

Alex, 41 years old, is the son of European immigrants.

He had left his wife. Sarah, to whom he had been mar-
ried for over two decades, as well as his two sons, ages
18 and 17, some three months before he came to my
office. He reported deep sadness, anxiety, and a disqui-
eting sense of "things being not the way they were
supposed to be " Alex and his wife had talked before
the separation. Both had agreed that the marriage had
been essentially "dead" for close to 10 years. The
prospect of continuing this relationship after their
children left home was frightening to both of them.
Sarah, still living in the family home and seeing her
sons on an almost daily basis, had tolerated the subse-
quent separation well She maintained a cordial,
although emotionally boundaried relationship with
Alex, and had even begun to date upon occasion. It was
Alex who showed up at the door, overwrought and
emotionally depleted after several days without sleep,
asking to return home. Reluctantly, out of a sense of
caring and concern, Sarah agreed. Now, several weeks
after his return home, Alex feels some measure of relief.
He long ago caught up on his sleep, and he feels com-
fortable with familiar furniture and the sounds and
smells of family life Yet, in our most recent sessions,
Alex has shared with me a deep sense of regret, almost a
self-loathing for as he put it, "letting myself down."

The Pull Back; The Push Forward

A common phenomena when a man experiences a relationship separation, and is faced with the tasks of mourning this
loss, is to be either regressively pulled back into the old relationship or prematurely propelled into a new one. Certainly, relationship separation can be a time of individual growth and change.
And either or both partners may consider returning to the relationship for very good and healthy reasons Indeed, much of my
clinical practice is devoted to helping couples in troubled relationships work through their difficulties and move to a deeper and
more satisfactory level of relating. This type of a return to an "old
relationship" is not what I am referring to when I discuss a
"regressive return" to the relationship By regressive, I mean the
seeking of refuge out of pain and confusion over a relationship
separation This return is not borne of hope for positive change

and a commitment to work on sustaining it into the future, but rather is based on fear, dependency, and longing. Having struggled with such dilemmas myself, I realize that knowing oneself well enough to begin to differentiate our healthy from our less healthy motives is a difficult, often almost impossible task. This task is made all the more problematic when choosing to leave a marriage means a separation from our children, as well as from our former partner.

Many a man has found himself using the energy of a new relationship to help pull him out of the throes of a marital connection that he no longer finds tolerable. Another common pattern is being propelled into a new relationship, sometimes even into a new family, shortly after a divorce, in an attempt to reconstitute the structure and the ''emotional holding'' of an intact family situation.

> *Ed, a well dressed and meticulously groomed bank officer, walked into my office hesitatingly. He suggested that he wasn't sure he should be there. The problem was, said Ed, ''that I keep making poor choices.'' He shared that his third marriage was in serious trouble because of what he called his wife's ''compulsive shopping.'' Ed detailed a sad story in which he had taken on additional responsibilities at work and had even taken on a side job, preparing taxes, in order to try and pay the household bills as they kept mounting. I inquired about his previous marriages and found out that Ed's first wife abused prescription medications, resulting in her emotional and physical deterioration; and that a second wife ''played around,'' despite Ed's pleas for her to stop and his attempts to make the relationship work. While outwardly blaming his former spouses, both of Ed's previous marriages ended with him feeling like he had failed, as if his competency and manhood had been challenged. Each time, he was eager to ''leave the past behind'' him and ''start over.'' It was only after a period of time, during which we ex-plored his ''self-sacrificing,'' codependent relationship behavior, his view of his role in relationships, and the connection this had to growing up in a chaotic, alco-holic home, that Ed began to look at himself and con-sider his contribution to his marital problems. In time,*

> *Ed began to attend appropriate 12-step meetings and work a conscientious program of both self-examination and healthy self-care. Shortly thereafter, Ed's wife began her own treatment with another therapist and began to understand and change her dysfunctional behavior.*

Shame and Guilt: Again the Twin Demons

Virtually no man I have ever worked with, or for that matter, no man that I have ever known (myself included), leaves a marital relationship without a great deal of guilt and a deep sense of shame over abandoning his socially prescribed role of protector and provider. Even in those cases where we are the ones left, there is deep guilt and shame in not meeting the expectation of the provider and protector role, mingled with the brutal sting of relationship rejection. Indeed, while financial issues and the practical concerns of continuing consistent parenting often are factors, I believe it is the perceived failure of the man as a provider and protector that results in many men leaving the family home during a marital separation while his spouse remains. In those cases where a father's relationship with his children has been positive prior to a relationship split, often being outside the home, away from familiar sources of identity and esteem, leads to a shame reaction of major proportions. We know that shame, if deep enough, can lead to "cut off" relationships, and that this failure to maintain close contact with children may result in more intense feelings of shame, unworthiness, and failure during contact with them.

I have little doubt that the phenomenon of the "deadbeat Dad" (an explicitly shaming and humiliating term), is an accurate interpretation of reality in some cases. My own experience suggests that these unfortunate circumstances often stem from shame-driven "cut-off" relationships and profound rage and resentment at the distorted remnants of the once honored provider and protector role, that of being primarily a source of financial supplies. If this observation has some merit, if only for a sizable minority of divorced men disconnected from their children, then the implications are considerable. This would suggest that, for them, resolving this problem is less a matter of applying sanctions and threatening public humiliation than it is a matter of assisting them to work through their guilt, shame, and rage at the outcome of a divorce process that they may have dimly understood and certainly emotionally mismanaged.

The "Second Parent"

Often, divorce will stimulate old feelings surrounding a child's early powerful connection to his or her mother. Following birth, fathers may feel very much "outside" the emotional and physical relationship between mother and child, very much the "second parent." Under the divisive stress of divorce, a fracture may occur along an emotional fault line dating back to when we experienced ourselves as the less important, less involved, less necessary parent. This self-perception of being the "second parent" can become yet another wedge between our children and ourselves. It can cause us to undervalue our importance as an emotional nurturer and propel us toward an unnecessarily incomplete or distant parenting role.

To successfully understand and negotiate the emotional perils of divorce and the loss that occurs as a result of the change in our relationships with our children, it is not enough to understand attachment, loss and separation, and the special nature of the divorce trauma. *Who we are in the context of these events is critically important, as well.* Therefore, we must also address our own, often early, personal experiences that color our later life and complicate our reaction to relationship separation.

Five

Complications

"I wasn't there that morning
When my father passed away
I didn't get to tell him
All the things I had to say.
I think I caught his spirit
Later that same year.
I'm sure I heard his echo
In my baby's newborn tears.
I just wish I could have told him
In the living years."

-- *The Living Years*, Mike and the Mechanics

"We carry around as men a "wounded father" inside:
A distorted sense of manhood,
and ourselves as defective, empty, or angry and demanding,
judgmental and critical;
a belief that manhood has little to give emotionally,
rooted in the experience of our fathers;
a conviction that women alone can give and receive love directly.
When a man has turned too often to women for help
without also finding support from men,
he may naturally come to feel that women
are the repositories of affection and caring."

-- Samuel Osherson, Ph.D., *"Wrestling With Love"*

It was six weeks shy of my 15th birthday. The night air
was cold and damp, and the New York streets slick with light rain
as my mother and I ambled panic-stricken down the sidewalk in
front of our house. I had been roused from my sleep less than
an hour earlier by my mother's frantic cries to seek help from
neighbors. My father was having an "attack" like the ones he

had suffered over two years before. Never quite sure what his ailment was, we learned to live in anxious anticipation of the return of the illness that rendered my father, an otherwise self-sufficient and very controlled man, unconscious and enfeebled. Yet, this time was different. My father's breathing labored and eventually stopped, punctuated only by occasional deep, convulsive gasps that shook his vomit-soaked body. My younger brother, just 9 years old the day before, stayed in his bed, perhaps out of a sense of the dread that lay beyond his room and no doubt paralyzed by a child's dim realization that his world was being shaken to its foundation.

"I think he's dead," I said to my mother, in my most practiced, pseudo-adult tone as we proceeded down the street, desperately escaping for only a few moments the gathering crowd, chaos, and sense of complete impotence that had invaded our home. It must have been then that my father, surrounded by neighbors, but not family, puked out his last bit of life.

Fifteen years later, virtually to the day, as Spring beckoned through the snow of the Rocky Mountain Winter, my daughter was born. There had been much talk that she might be born on the same day of the year that my father had died. Indeed, as much as my rational mind argued against burdening a child with such a notion, there was a deep, emotional resonance that occurred with her birth. My sense of wonder at the miracle that was her was made all the more profound as my becoming a father reverberated with that still grief-stricken part of me that lost my own a decade and a half before. Through the years, I have struggled to maintain a loving and consistent relationship with my daughter through my own divorce, remarriage, and the formation of the new family that we are a part of. I have also struggled not to burden her with her father's deep reservoir of grief over an attachment torn asunder when he was 15 or the power of his profound joy and wonder at an attachment made a decade and a half later. And so it is with my daughter, and the others that I have been able to love, that I have come to accept that so much of what I struggle with, so much of what I fear, is still rooted in a cold, damp, senseless night in New York, now some 25 years ago.

Our own histories, our loves and losses, as well as our

triumphs and disappointments, provide the canvas on which our current relationships are painted. Perhaps most importantly, our early experience with parenting figures significantly influences, for better or for worse, our capacity to form satisfying attachments with others and to successfully tolerate and manage loss. As a general rule, a person with an early history of firm attachments and gentle separations and returns will internalize a firm foundation for dealing with both relationship development and separation. If there is a relatively secure attachment with a parenting figure, and ordinary, non-traumatic experience in separating and reconnecting, a child develops a capacity for firm attachments and an ability to tolerate separation from important others. While a person with this early developmental experience may grieve over a loss, this grieving is more likely to be successful and uncomplicated. Those individuals with early backgrounds which result in insecure, anxious or ambivalent attachments are likely to have more difficulty tolerating relationship separation or loss.

Art, 29 years old and separated from his wife, was referred to me for evaluation of what his family physician believed were "panic attacks." After meeting with him and taking a thorough history, it became clear that Art's early years were marked by much disruption. Born when his mother was only 17 years old, Art was initially raised by his grandparents while his mother lived in an apartment nearby. When he was almost two years old, Art's grandmother was killed in an accident; and he began to live with his mother in her apartment. Depressed at her own mother's death, drinking heavily, and moving from relationship to relationship, Art's mother tended to be emotionally unresponsive and openly neglectful of his needs. Shortly before his fourth birthday, Art's mother made a suicide attempt while heavily intoxicated. Subsequently, Art was placed in the custody of the State and was put in a foster home. While the foster home placement was a relatively positive one, Art dimly remembers feeling very fearful of being sent away again and also recalls being deeply concerned over the whereabouts of his mother. After about a year, Art was returned to his mother, who, by that time, had stopped drinking, had sought treatment, and was working regularly. Shortly thereafter, she married, provid-

*ing a relatively stable and dependable family structure
for Art throughout his growing up years.*

*At age 21, Art met his future wife and began what was to
be basically an unhappy relationship for both partners.
Over the years, it seemed that Art's wife would threaten
to leave him every few months, resulting in his pleas for
her to stay with him. A month before coming to see me
with his panic attacks, Art's wife made good on her
threats and finally left, taking with her their four year
old daughter.*

*Art experienced severe anxiety when he went to bed
alone. He called his wife incessantly and often drove by
his former home late at night. On the few occasions he
saw his daughter, he was overwhelmed with anxiety
when it was time to return her to her mother. It was
after one such return that Art began to experience chest
pains and was taken to the emergency room by a friend
from work.*

*A medical evaluation proved negative, and Art was
subsequently referred to my office. While Art initially
benefitted from the use of medication prescribed by his
physician, as well as specific techniques to deal with his
severe anxiety, it was over the course of several months
of therapy that Art came to understand the powerful
effect his early life had on his relationship behavior and
his reaction to separation.*

The Shadow of Past Attachments

During vulnerable developmental periods, such as childhood or adolescence, when we are normally and naturally consolidating our sense of separateness and our ability to care for
ourselves away from caretakers, traumatic loss may cast a long
shadow on our future relationship life. Our capacity to form new
relationships, the types of partners we are drawn to, our emotional
reaction to relationship loss such as divorce, may all be influenced
by such experiences. In my own life, the death of my father, and
the upheaval that occurred in my family following his death, have
had a pervasive effect on my later relationship life. My reaction

to the birth of my daughter, my divorce, the nature of my relationship with my daughter, my desire to enter a new relationship, my relationship with my present wife and our other two children, all have been impacted by the upheaval in my life 25 years ago. Paradoxically, denial of the influence of past losses results in their having a particularly powerful effect, as our unprocessed grief is "acted out" beyond our awareness in current relationships.

My own personal journey has involved grieving my past losses, understanding how the losses of yesterday impact me today, and trying to make choices that move me toward secure, meaningful attachments in the present. Thus, I have come to believe that unless we grieve, we are destined to repeat, to try and reach some resolution of past losses in the here and now.

Children of Divorce Grown Up

Many men have experienced a parental divorce while growing up. For most, the divorce remains the major disruption of their childhood, a coming apart that forever colors their experiencing of relationship connections. Adult participation in a failed marriage, regardless of who initiates the split, threatens to reactivate the old wounds of childhood. Some men vow never to allow their marriage to end. This may be a desperate attempt to avoid anything that could resonate with their painful past. Some employ a defensive strategy in their marriages, never fully investing their emotional energy into the relationship; engaging instead in a self-fulfilling prophecy that hastens an "inevitable" split.

Many men who experienced a parental divorce when young, unless they come to understand and work through the particular circumstances of that early experience, will go on to form adult relationships in the shadow of their original, ruptured family structure. If their own marriage is severely stressed, if separation and divorce become a possibility or a reality, old issues, often long buried and denied, may emerge. For those whose marriage was an unconscious attempt to heal the damage of the past, a separation and divorce process may be particularly painful. The guilt and shame in relationship to our own children may seem overwhelming, as we come to realize that we may have unwittingly participated in causing them the same pain that hurt us most deeply.

Boys Without Men

The fact of the matter is that for the overwhelming majority of men that experienced a parental divorce while growing up, their father was the parent who left home, became less available, and went on with a life that often did not include them. In some cases, fathers lost contact with them altogether. These boys were often raised by their mothers in homes dramatically impacted-- emotionally, financially, and structurally-- by the absence of Dad. At least implicitly, and often explicitly, fathers were blamed and derided for their abandonment of their family, their failure to maintain contact, and their frequent lack of financial support. The larger culture, likewise, has chronically sent shaming and vilifying messages about fathers who are no longer with their families.

In such families, surrounded by women and learning to respond to women's needs, these "feminized men" (Kipnis, 1991) may grow up with a biased view of their own masculinity, adopting a feminized emotional system and world-view based more on maintaining harmony with women and meeting women's needs than on asserting themselves and using their energy to get their own needs met. Every boy in such a family situation, no matter how emotionally sturdy and eager to learn how to be a man, is at risk of internalizing the idea of a man as abandoning and fundamentally "bad." Paradoxically, every boy raised in such a situation is also at risk of developing a defensively hyper-masculine, almost caricatured version of "being a man" in an attempt to manage self-esteem and avoid a sense of domination by women. No such boy, now a man, can deny otherwise warded-off feelings of shame, guilt, and simple self-loathing when he sees himself participating in breaking up his family and disrupting his relationship to his own children. I cannot count the men who have come to my office and have muttered in self-condemnation, "I'm just like Dad." Indeed, even those who may have sincerely attempted to manage their separation and divorce with respect for their spouse and commitment to their children, may experience these extremely negative thoughts and feelings.

Disconnected Dads

If fathers were absent, as in the case of divorce with paternal distancing, or (as in my case) the death of a father, we are left with the virtually impossible task of separating our either idealized or devalued sense of who our father was from the reality of his existence. In the end, we must come to grips with who *we are*, coming to understand our woundedness at our father's absence or unavailability. Yet, not all our fathers were physically absent. Many fathers were emotionally unavailable, even if they were physically present. So many of our fathers were raised in a generation which lured them far away from home and children, into a separate world of work. While work outside the home has historically been the province of men, 20th century industrialization, technical advance, and specialization compartmentalized the world of work. For men, the result was an increased dichotomy between home and work. When they were home, our fathers may have been depleted by work, struggling to maintain a safe haven behind a newspaper or in front of the television in order to "refuel." If home was the province of women, and father pulled back from an active role, both dependence on women and the perceived domestic marginality of men was all too obvious. If administering discipline was Dad's job, then perhaps the only reliable connection we had with him was intermittent, angry exchanges tinged with shame.

Our fathers' strong suit for many of us was the world of "things" rather than relationships. Our connection with him was often about doing, fixing, completing, and competing. It is these images of father, made more powerful by virtue of our concentrated exposure to him for brief periods of time, that we carry with us. I remember clearly my father, walking away from the fresh gravesite at his father's funeral, teetering in the emotional netherworld between "control" and "tears." I remember thinking it odd that I never did see him really cry that day, the day he buried *his father*. Now, as I remember clearly my father's face, holding back tears, I understand and think it much less odd. He was in charge of "arrangements." He had to perform, not grieve.

Relationships with Mothers

Our relationships with our mothers may cause us difficulty, not only because of their likely prominence as the more available and often influential parent, but also because their softness, nurturance, and consistent presence may call into question our sense of independence, power, and developing sense of masculinity. Contact with our mothers in the absence of father carries with it the risk of fear of domination, and a simultaneous risk of adoption of a feminized emotional and need-fulfilling system. There may also be an increased discomfort of attraction to mother without an obvious male figure to protect us from too strong an awareness of our unconscious longings. Father-absence deprives us of an alternative nurturer that is rougher, less enveloping, and separate from Mom. For some men, this quandary of wanting nurturance from women, but fearing domination by them, continues well into adulthood.

Who We Were in our Families

As powerful as the social and cultural forces are that move a man into a heroic, controlling, yet emotionally restricted role, more immediate forces impact us as well. The role we played in our families impacts us mightily. We may be a family hero, accepting responsibility at an early age and forfeiting our own needs and wants to the demands of the family system, or a "scapegoat," always getting into trouble to take the family's attention off of deeper problems. Whatever the role, we are always in danger of carrying these roles into the families we create as adults. Often, we may be the unaware recipient of our parents' unresolved issues as we "act out" or reenact old scripts in our current life that were not adequately worked through in the families we grew up in

Wes, who identifies himself as an adult child of an alcoholic, essentially raised his younger brothers and sisters after his father left the family and his mother worked. A gifted athlete, Wes attended college where he met the woman who was to become his wife In thinking back, Wes is unable to identify the exact time when he realized his wife was chemically dependent. He does recall working two jobs and then coming home to take care of his own children, often without the help of his wife Despite several attempts to stop drinking, both in treatment and through Alcoholics Anonymous, his wife s alcoholism remained

*active, while Wes accepted more and more responsibility in the
running of the family. Not surprisingly, the relationship eventually ended in divorce. Now, with shared custody of his children,
Wes is still the consummate caretaker, carrying much more than
his share of the burden of parenting the children and often
spending time at his former spouse's home working on her car
or doing repairs around the house.*

A repeating of old dynamics may appear in other ways.
For instance, a man may make a precipitous decision to leave a
troubled relationship because he unconsciously resonates with
the deep pain and shame his hard-working, long-suffering father
experienced in his parents' emotionally barren marriage. In this
respect, we may, in a sense, experience our parents' (unrealized)
divorce.   Alternatively, a man may go through all sorts of
emotional gymnastics to keep his marriage together in an attempt
to heal the wound of his parents' fractured marriage.

Healing and Moving On

Some of you might think, having read this far, that the
task of grieving the losses of divorce and working toward a
continuing, meaningful relationship with our children is a task so
arduous, so complicated, so haunted by the hand of the past and
plagued by the pain of the present, that the effort may not be worth
it. To be sure, I cannot promise you progress without pain.
Indeed, it is conventional wisdom that ''The only way out of our
pain is through it.'' As a matter of fact, it is often our attempt to
avoid pain at all costs that leaves us empty and alone. I *can* assure
you, with a strong measure of confidence, that the task will be
worth it. You will come to understand yourself and your
relationship life as never before, and your relationship with your
children, while changed forever, will develop into a sturdy and
meaningful connection that continually enriches your life with the
bittersweet challenge of fatherhood.

PART II

**Healing, Growth and Renewal:
Staying Connected and Moving On**

*We cannot solve life's problems except
by solving them. This statement may seem
idiotically tautological or self-evident,
yet it is seemingly beyond the comprehension
of much of the human race. This is because
we must accept responsibility for a problem
before we can solve it.*

-- M. Scott Peck, *The Road Less Traveled*

Six

Taking Inventory

It is true that the present is powerfully shaped by the past.
But it is also true that the circumstances of every stage
of development can shake up and revise the old arrangements.
And it is true that insight at any age can free us from
singing the same sad songs again.

-- Judith Viorst, *Necessary Losses*

In a simpler, ideal world, as losses occur in our lives, we would grieve them vigorously and completely, and then move on. However, the world in which we live is neither simple nor ideal. The grief process is uneven and sloppy, proceeding in fits and starts, and occasionally stalling. Traumatic losses often occur when we are young, without the sense of separation, the cognitive development, or the emotional maturity necessary to move beyond them. We may be left with significant vulnerability to future losses. The families we were raised in may not have afforded us the modeling or support necessary to develop healthy access to our feelings. As men, we likely received powerful messages from parents, friends, and spouses, as well as society at large, that we should endure, if not ignore, painful losses. Over the course of our lives, so many of us are left with a deep, well-contained reservoir of raw, unprocessed, accumulated grief. When we experience a major loss, such as divorce, we may be moved either toward more denial and compartmentalization of our pain, or toward a frightening and confusing pouring forth of powerful feelings. Often we experience wild fluctuations as we experience our pain, and then suddenly back away from it, only to swing back toward it again. Unless we have a sense of what our cumulative losses were and how they affected us, we may have little chance of understanding our grief reactions in the here and now, leaving us at high risk for a dysfunctional response to current relationship loss. It is this dysfunctional response, often rooted in the disruptions of the past, which may stunt our capacity to care for ourselves and to maintain a meaningful relationship with our children following divorce.

The Loss Inventory

When I speak of taking inventory of our losses, I do not mean filling out a particular form or following a rigid outline. Some of us do best writing long, detailed paragraphs. Others of us are more impressionistic, jotting down the core words and symbols which convey to us the emotional meaning of another time and place. A "timeline" detailing the types and timing of losses during our lifetime may work for many. Using a straightline graph, we can develop a chronological perspective, allowing us to see patterns in our losses and our reaction to them. We are much better off not simply listing our losses, however, since this tends to reinforce attempts to remain emotionally distant from them. A notebook or journal that you use for no purpose other than recording your loss inventory works best. At first, resolve to keep this writing to yourself, since for many of us, sharing our pain and our secrets may bring up a great deal of shame. At some point in this process, however, most of us will find that the emotional intensity experienced may require finding a safe individual or group setting in which to share these feelings and receive feedback.

Simply moving our thoughts and feelings from our minds and hearts to paper, no matter how clumsily or incompletely, forces us to confront and process our reality in a different way. For most, spending some time each day over a period of a few weeks is a valuable approach, although different styles may fit different men. As each section is written, often it is helpful to leave it alone for a few hours or a day and then return to read it. Reading the section aloud, as well as to ourselves, forces us to hear our own words, making their meaning yet more real. For those of us who have become expert at repressing, minimizing, and "putting away" our most painful experiences, this process forces us to reconsider and, perhaps, revisit our losses, often resulting in long overdue emotional discharge. For those of us who experience our feelings very strongly, with little sense of the reasons for their intensity, writing allows us to make mental connections between our experiences and our emotional reactions, as well as giving us a sense of containment. If we tend to be emotionally reactive, we may back away from potentially painful situations, such as discussing a relationship separation with a spouse or explaining divorce to children. The containment that writing affords us provides an opportunity to process our feelings, make sense of them, and then behave with intentionality rather than just defensively. Safe, constructive feedback at this stage may prove essential for our further growth.

What to Include

We must cast our net broadly when trying to recapture the past losses, separations, and disruptions that may have impacted us. We must learn the skill of being a "fly on the wall" in our own lives and begin to recognize influential events from outside our own perspective. For instance, if we experienced our father's absence or our mother's illness and hospitalization as a "normal and natural" part of life, we may not easily develop the perspective necessary to understand the impact of these events on us. However, if we pull out of our subjective view for a moment, we can recognize parental absence or emotional distance as being influential factors in virtually anyone's life. Conversely, we must also develop the capacity to acknowledge the impact of events on us, even if similar events have had little apparent impact on others. For instance, most children experience a geographic move. For many, such a move may have been managed with relatively little difficulty. Nonetheless, an event that has apparently little enduring impact on others may have a significant effect on us, depending on our age, stage of development, and the availability of consistent family support.

In considering childhood losses, separations, and interruptions, we must adopt the perspective of the child, a perspective in which time and distance had much different meanings than our adult conceptions. Examples of childhood events include (but in no way are limited to): our own early illness or hospitalization, parental illness or hospitalization, parental death or divorce, the loss of a beloved grandparent, conflict in our parents' relationship, threatened or actual abandonment, parental alcoholism or mental illness, the death of a friend, loss of a pet, geographic moves, changing schools, or exposure to frequent discussion of a parent's loss experiences and fears.

While many of the events noted above are also significant in adolescence, the stresses of this stage typically involve attempts to separate from home and parents, managing a developing sense of sexuality, connecting with peers, and consolidating a sense of identity. Thus, the disruptions and losses more typical of adolescence often involve traumatic sexual experiences, confusion over the handling of sexuality in a relationship, intense and unstable peer attachments, parental rejection due to attempts to separate or due to parental discomfort with developing sexuality, early pregnancies and premature parental responsibilities, terminated pregnancies, academic difficulties or failures, or losing a friend in an accident.

Approaching adulthood brings with it more serious, stable relationships and the potential for the loss of more enduring connections, such as marriage. Career strivings may be interrupted by academic or vocational failure. Financial losses may be felt for the first time. We experience the final loss of the opportunity for childhood dependence. It is in young adulthood that we strongly sense that we live in a world of limited possibilities, are hit with the awareness of aging parents, and are given the responsibility of caring for the next generation.

Later losses include confronting our own aging and physical deterioration, the later growth of our children and their gradual moving away from home, our own parents' illnesses and impending deaths, and the disquieting awareness that we are the next generation to move on.

What Does All this Have to Do With "Now"?

Recognizing the hurts and losses of the past is often helpful in releasing old feelings and beginning to lessen the burden of unresolved grief. However, it finds its real value in helping us understand our reactions and by informing our actions in the present. We may find that our apparent inattention to divorce and separation from our children is a part of an entrenched pattern of "turning down the volume" on our feelings. In fact, we may diminish our emotional reactivity so much that our feelings no longer serve their survival function of warning us when our primary attachments are threatened.

Chris, a bright and ambitious salesman, was known for managing his work life with a capacity to shrug off disappointments and setbacks. With a coping style initially learned in his tumultuous, alcoholic family and galvanized during experiences in high school athletics and a hitch in the Marine Corps., Chris reached adulthood with the commitment that any setback, any loss, must be handled with an immediate and tenacious attempt to move beyond it. Indeed, I frankly doubt that Chris would have even considered coming to my office had not his coworker and best friend insisted on it.

Chris, left by his wife of two years just 45 days earlier, had thrown himself into a round of excessive work and involvement with other women. Only twice had he tried to see his one year old daughter, and he rarely even inquired about her during the few times he spoke to his wife during the separation. Reluctant to consider a second appointment with me, and then reluctant to consider a third, Chris gradually began to understand the origins of his coping style. Only then did he slowly begin to think about the losses in the family in which he grew up and about the reality of the likely loss of his marriage and his relationship with his young child.

Some of us may be surprised to find that deep, unquenchable grief, stimulated by divorce, may have more to do with the accumulated power of past rejections, separations, and losses than it does with the reality of our current situation. We may come to understand our rage, our sadness, our shame, our guilt, or our sense of emptiness in a new light.

Ben, a likeable, 53 year old, grey-haired university professor, sought out therapy three months after reaching a mutual decision with his wife to separate after over 30 years of marriage. With three grown children, continued residence in his home, a successful teaching and writing career, numerous long-term friends, and continued contact with his wife at family gatherings, Ben was at a loss to explain the extremity of his shame, sadness, and rage in reaction to the separation. Most disturbing to Ben was his unaccountable rage towards his wife. At the time he came to see me, Ben was having trouble falling asleep despite being very tired, his appetite was inconsistent, and he had little interest in recreational pursuits or in seeing his friends. His occasional glass of wine had turned into a daily occurrence. For the first time in his university career, Ben's work began to suffer, and students began to comment on the inconsistency of the quality of his lectures.

Although I was aware that Ben's own parents divorced when he was nine years old, he initially was unable or unwilling to discuss this in very much detail. Several sessions later, Ben began to talk about the shame and emotional havoc which surrounded his parents' dissolved marriage and his father's emotional decline following the split. He talked about seeing his father as weak and unable to cope with life, as well as of his own difficulty feeling good about being male. He mentioned how he began to see his mother as uncaring and hurtful to his father. Ben, over time, began to see his marriage as his own attempt to "fix" the past and leave his pain behind him. His role as a tenured professor, his stable marriage, his successful adult children, all served to allow Ben to avoid confronting his unresolved pain. Now, outside the structure of his marital relationship, hurt and confusion over four decades old began to surface in his current life.

Clearly, it is critically important to understand and grieve the hurt and losses of the past. Yet, so many of us struggle with experiencing and expressing our feelings. Raised too often in a context where emotional expression was the province of women, where experiencing and expressing feelings was a source of confusion, shame, and humiliation, we must search for an authentic male emotionality

<u>Seven</u>

Taming the Demons: Authentic Male Emotionality

"Many of the attributes we had come to feel ashamed of are actually fine qualities that have been misunderstood or misdirected. We gave one another a lot of support for experimenting with new styles of relating to life. We came to believe that in their core men are not only good, but noble and magical as well."

-- Aaron Kipnis, Ph.D., *Knights Without Armor*.

<u>Common Male Emotional Styles</u>

The usual choices left to men regarding how to manage their feelings in the face of relationship demands are typically extreme and stereotyped ones. One role, the "hero", the protector and provider, focuses on the needs of others while sacrificing one's own, in return for thanks and idealization. This style essentially leaves us isolated from ourselves and others. The emotionally repressed, logical "problem-solver" is too safely solution-oriented, missing out on the rich process, the color, the pain and passion of intimate connection. The "feminized" man is exquisitely sensitive to the needs of women in his life, while largely unaware of his own. All too often he carries an angry and derogating attitude toward his own maleness. The "macho", hypermasculine role is but a defensive caricature of true tough-ness, courage, and competence, often leaving in its wake a trail of emotional abuse, overdrinking, and violence.

As the defensive nature of these styles indicates, the damage done to the male psyche, to his sense of emotional balance and wholeness, over the last several generations has been enormous. Alienated from parts of himself by a technological age, acculturated into a corporate ethos, separated from home and family by the world of work "out there", deprived of emotionally available men and raised by women, numbed by the slaughter and senselessness of declared and undeclared wars, left without children in the case of divorce, and confused by rapid political, social, and economic changes which daily threaten to redefine his place in the world, we cannot be surprised that he has sought refuge in these distorted, extreme styles. They offer the illusory promise of a sense of self, predictability, and meaning. It is clear, however, that the emotional systems of each of these roles are poorly equipped to manage the tasks of true intimacy, mature commitment, and responsibility to self and others. No doubt it is the inflexibility and limited nature of these emotional coping styles that contribute to the very relationship problems that result in divorce.

These same emotional styles leave us further upset and disconnected at the time of relationship separation and divorce, for each one carries within it the seeds of self-defeat. The "hero", protector, and provider, must face the deep shame and guilt of failure. The logical, emotionally repressed "organization man" moves further away from people under the stress of loss, filling his life with the temporary balm of a focus on things. The feminized man suffers self-derogation stemming from an internalized image of men as abandoning, abusive, or neglectful. The hypermasculine male, valuing action at the expense of self-reflection, finds himself repeating the painful mistakes of the past, in an unending cycle of aggressive acting out. The paradox is that parts of each style, the heroic, the sensitive, the logical, and the active, when tempered into the alloy of authentic wholeness, can offer us the best hope of realizing our full emotional potential.

Moving Towards Wholeness

Many of us have adopted a coping style as a matter of actual or perceived emotional survival. Regardless of what style we chose to emphasize, we tended to "put away", deny, or repress other parts. The feminized male tends to deride assertive action or deemphasize cold logic. The hypermasculine male is unaware or deeply ashamed of his sensitive or logical parts. The logical man shuns feeling or assertive action. The hero rarely looks into himself, so absorbed is he in seeing himself reflected in the eyes of others. Our capacity to grieve our losses, to maintain connections with our children, to claim our birthright of full emotionality, depends on our realizing and developing these lost parts of ourselves. To be able to live with joy and sadness, grief and hope, passion and reason, ferocity and gentleness; this is the promise of authentic male emotionality.

Authentic Male Emotionality, Not Androgyny

In recent years, a frequently endorsed goal for men and women has been that of *androgeny*-- flexibility and comfort with both male and female typical behaviors, roles, and relationship styles. This is *not* what is being suggested by authentic masculine emotionality. Instead of a neutered homogenization of styles, authentic male emotionality refers to a way of relating to self and others that honors and promotes, rather than derides, the healthy expression of the characteristically masculine: ferocity, strength, commitment to principle, physical protectiveness, and productivity. Authentic masculinity does not equate a man's expression of these emotions with danger, but rather recognizes the value of genuine passion, productive anger, healthy pride, and focused power. Authentic male emotionality allows for the experiencing and expression of deep grief. Finally, authentic male emotionality includes tenderness, gentle nurture, and empathic connection, but not as a defensive stance or as a sanctuary from our anger and passion. This approach recognizes social and political equality between men and women, yet does not require emotional sameness.

In the Presence of Others

Since we lost part of our emotional potential in the families in which we grew up, and during our experience with society at large, recovering our emotional potential must occur in the presence of others, as well. Usually, we have deep shame over the hidden or undeveloped parts of ourselves. It is in the presence of others, especially other men, that we can develop our lost emotionality. As we see different aspects of ourselves reflected in the eyes of others (perhaps for the first time), our shame lessens, we feel more whole, more expressive. It is with caring friends, mentors, older males, or peers in a men's group that we have our chance to heal.

Dan, raised since he was seven years old by his mother and his two older sisters, sat in group, week after week, always sensitive to the needs of the other men in group. He was always understanding, always psychologically-minded, yet rarely in touch with his own feelings related to the losses of his divorce, including the loss of significant contact with his children. Despite much attention from the group, Dan stated that he "accepted" the divorce. He said that he "understood" his wife's position. Then, unexpectedly, one day in group, while listening to the painful story of another man who had lost contact with his own father when he was only five, Dan began to experience the buried feelings from his own childhood loss, as well as the "here-and-now" losses he was experiencing. To the surprise of the other men in group, Dan's irritation turned to anger, and then his anger turned to rage, as he stamped his feet and slammed his fist into the palm of the other hand. "I hate her, I hate her," he kept repeating. As Dan's rage began to fade, his sadness began to surface. Dan started to sob. . .and to heal.

Our defensive styles, our shame, our guilt, all leave us isolated, separated from the very sources of support and validation that offer us healing. To seize the opportunity to heal, we must face one of the most difficult set of tasks involved in reclaiming our emotional wholeness-- knowing when we need help, knowing where to look for help, and, finding the courage to ask for it.

Eight

Asking for and Getting Help

*"I always felt like I was alone; really like I had to be alone.
That was how I was supposed to be. I tried to go through my divorce
alone; I tried to take care of my kids alone; I thought I could snap
out of my depression on my own. It's almost like I thought I might
die if I asked for help. What a relief to know that I am not alone.
Now I understand that going it alone was part of the problem, not
part of the solution.''*

      -- Reggie, a 28 year old, former professional football player,
*discussing his realization of how his difficulty asking for help
complicated his divorce experience and interfered with his own
growth.*

      The exaggerated, extreme emotional coping styles discussed in the last chapter all have something in common. Yet ultimately they leave us separated and alienated from ourselves and from others. We need to connect with others in order to heal and develop the lost parts of our emotional selves. We need to restore what Kaufman (1985) calls the "interpersonal bridge" of empathic connection, in order to see ourselves, *all* of ourselves, reflected and validated in the eyes of others. It is only then that we seem to be able to give ourselves "permission" to be who we truly are.

      All of us need this type of connection. If we are fortunate, we get it in large doses when we are young, from our parents and other caregivers. In the best of cases, we continue to get it in age-appropriate ways as we mature. But if we are less fortunate, if parental attention was absent, inconsistent, or shaming, or our parents were too self-involved to reflect back to us the sense of "specialness" so important in building self-esteem, we may find ourselves troubled adults. We have difficulty feeling good about ourselves or reaching out for help in a time of vulnerability. Of course, periods of emotional vulnerability are precisely the circumstances that make it imperative to connect with others. And we need not necessarily have deep childhood wounds in order to have difficulty connecting with others. Lifelong learning in a society which values men's independence over our connectedness, action over self-reflection, and competition over cooperation, is enough to leave many of us feeling alone, alienated, and confused.

Men Helping Men

There is much written about the necessity of men seeking out other men in order to heal. This is because for many of us, a core issue is our reliance on a limited or distorted idea of maleness. For some men, asking women for help at a time of relationship separation may stimulate deep shame over dependency or neediness. We may seek the comfort of women without being able to ask for their help. Particularly at a time of relationship separation or divorce, many men may feel too emotionally raw, hurt, angry, or victimized to risk a potentially healing connection with a woman

There is some irony to this predicament of finding ourselves isolated from others, particularly isolated from other men. Many of us have had very close relationships with male peers as boys and adolescents Indeed, many men report a strong bond, a real love relationship, with a boyhood chum This type of relationship is usually given up as a rite of passage when connections with women are pursued. Often, relationships with boyhood chums are very important and strongly missed by men, even after they engage in adult relationships with women. While our boyhood chums are gone, the opportunity to renew supportive and validating relationships with other men is not.

Who to Ask

We may be fortunate enough to have good male friends we can spend time with, and from whom we may receive comfort and support. For those of us with a "father wound," we may identify a mentor at work or at school, usually an older or more experienced, seasoned male Developing a relationship with such a man can pull us along the path of growth and maturation

I believe that the 12 Step concept of sponsorship, in its best sense, is a type of mentoring relationship. In a perverse act of fate, some of us have more direct access to our fathers now that we are adults than we did when we were children. The opportunity to talk about old hurts, understand the world from Dad's point of view, and develop a supportive relationship in the "here and now" can be a very healing one. Older, emotionally available males are a precious resource to men who are working to understand themselves, their past, and its impact on the present. Clearly, friendships with men tend to be difficult to cultivate, but can be a needed source of support and caring.

Can Men get it "Right"?

Much is said about men's difficulty with intimacy, with sharing and communication, and often with good reason. However, I believe that much of this criticism is misguided and based on the dominant, women's model of healthy intimacy, communication, and relationship-building. Generations of socialization and training in side-by-side work, warfare, and competition, have left many men with a male communication and bonding style that seems more indirect, less verbal, and often based on a common, shared activity. Half-sentences, nods of the head, intermittent connecting with a return to a joint focus, is the norm rather than the exception. A deepening of relationships, the development of a more flexible communication style, and working through fears of intimacy and exposure are, of course, worthy goals. However, it is a mistake to treat traditional male forms of communication as "second best." They are the authentic foundations upon which other skills must be built, not a problem to be overcome.

Even if we want to develop new ways of connecting with others and want to risk increased intimacy, we need a place to start; and the place to start is where we are at. Sitting with buddies watching a basketball game, or playing softball or going fishing, may seem to some like the antithesis of intimate connection. Yet, we can see how this type of relating is a reflection of our collective and individual pasts, a manner of relating that is thousands of years old and is bound up for many of us with the boyhood chumships of yesterday.

Blocks to Intimacy Among Men

Competition, the socially reinforced idea that this is a world of winners and losers, may leave us very wary of exposing ourselves to other men To leave ourselves vulnerable in some contexts--some athletic pursuits, warfare, corporate life--may mean sudden loss, even death To unlearn this defensiveness, this hypervigilance to threat, is a process that initially requires a leap of faith, even in the most benign situations. To risk sharing with other men usually requires us to acknowledge our fear and our shame, recognize where these painful feelings are coming from, and then going ahead with our attempt to connect nonetheless.

Perhaps less apparent is a fear that emotional intimacy between men suggests homosexuality. Most of us have been impacted by being raised in a largely homophobic society. For some, the boyhood taunts derisively suggesting homosexuality at signs of sensitivity, softness, or emotionality, are still very pow-erful when we get close to other men as adults. And do not men often confuse emotional intimacy with sexuality in their relation-ships with women, since this is the primary context in which they are expected to express their feelings? To be emotionally intimate, to feel connected, may bring up feelings usually re-served for relationships that also have a sexual component. Sorting these feelings out, deciding what types of emotional sharing and physical contact are comfortable in which types of relationships, is an important and necessary early stage in learn-ing to share and connect. And finally, if we do not experience ourselves as having effective boundaries--physical, interper-sonal, and emotional--being close can feel too threatening.

A Men's Group

For many, a men's group can become a place of healing and growth, a sanctuary where the echoes of yesterday's chumships and the cries of today's pain can be heard and validated. A group, whether it is a professionally facilitated therapy group, a leader-less support group, or a men's 12 Step group, develops a life and culture of its own. A group can offer a sense of safety and belonging, of comradeship and connection, beyond the sum of its individual relationships.

"My father was there for me when he wasn't drinking," said Carl, sharing with the other men in group his boyhood sense of his father. "The only problem was that he was almost always drinking," he added with false levity.

After a few awkward chuckles, Brian, divorced and a father of two young children, broke his silence. "I tried to squeeze as much as I could out of my relationship with my dad," he said. He added, "The times we went fishing or he took me to a ball game, or I got to go to work with him, those were pretty special to me. I wish I had more of those times with him. That's why I'm so damn determined to hang in there with my kids now."

"I had a dream about my father last week," added Sal, a 42 year old car salesman whose father had died when he was in high school. I dreamt that he hugged me, and then we walked through a door; and there were my kids, really young, playing on the floor. Dad looked at them and smiled, a real warm, satisfied smile, like he approved." Sal's eyes glistened as he continued, "It was like he was telling me that I had done good, like he was proud of me."

Can't Women Help?

It would be a grave disservice if I suggested that the only type of relationship in which a man can grow emotionally is with another man or with a group of men. My focus on men helping men comes from the important fact that many of us have a sense of maleness that is still incomplete, that lacks models of the full range of ways of being a man. Frequently, relationships with women pull us back into narrow, practiced roles, making change too scary or shame-provoking. This is not to say that some men may not be well-served by beginning their journey in the more familiar company of women. Nor is it to say that men who start to work on themselves in the context of relationships with other men will not need, at some point, to face their issues with women. This is particularly important in the case of men emerging from a divorce process. In therapy or counseling relationships, I have found that while men may initially prefer to work with a male therapist, over time gender differences among therapists seem to matter less, and skilled helpers of either gender that have faced and worked through their own issues can be of valuable and enduring assistance

What About Lawyers?

Most men that I work with very much want to avoid costly and lengthy entanglements. While I am certainly not an attorney and not qualified to dispense legal advice, my own bias is to assist men to work through their own feelings and unrecognized issues well enough to allow them to participate in the difficult process of developing a fair, mutually agreeable divorce settlement with a better chance of success. This includes child custody agreements. In an attempt to assist those I work with to avoid unnecessarily adversarial experiences, I often refer divorcing couples to professional mediators, skilled facilitators trained and experienced in dispute resolution and communication.

This having been said, however, I have found from the psychological/emotional perspective, that there are times to encourage individuals to seek legal advice. For instance, one such situation is when one partner is unwilling or unable to participate in a counseling or mediation process and communication is not forthcoming for an extended period of time. When feelings, words, or behaviors are out of control, when counseling or mediation has been ineffective and the situation may have become emotionally abusive or physically dangerous, I recommend that legal remedies be considered. I have found that attorneys may be particularly useful in helping us to set limits or boundaries that we are unable to set. Divorce is at best a very upsetting experience for children When parental conflict becomes deeply entrenched and harmful to our youngsters' welfare, firm legal support may be needed to move along the process.

Knowing When We are in Trouble

Significant emotional upset, explosive anger, sadness, anxiety, a sense of disquieting numbness or emptiness, and confusion, all may be part of a normal grieving process in response to relationship separation and divorce. Heavily involving oneself in work or exercise may be a healthy, if temporary, coping mechanism to get us through a difficult period. Grieving is not a clear, concise, easily defined phenomena, and there may be significant individual differences in grief responses. But there are (if sometimes subtle) qualitative differences between relatively healthy or benign grief-related thoughts, feelings, and coping behaviors and more dysfunctional emotional or behavioral health problems, such as a reliance on drugs or alcohol to "cope."

I begin to become concerned about someone that I am working with when he or she presents with a grief process that seems to be "stuck" for an extended period of time. As weeks or months pass, I look for some sort of process, some type of movement that gives an indication that an individual, in his or her own way, is advancing. Differentiating between grief and clinical depression has been a topic of discussion since the time of Freud. Clinical depression is present when expressed anger becomes painfully bottled up; when feelings of sadness become generalized and are not only related to the loss. It is present when a capacity to enjoy life despite the loss, if only for moments, becomes a pervasive sense of doom; when sadness is complicated by a sense of hopelessness. It is present when temporary physical complaints and changes in sleep pattern or appetite become chronic; when guilt and lowered self-esteem become ongoing and prevalent rather than temporary and specific to the loss. And, clearly it is present if a basic commitment to going on with one's life is threatened by thoughts or impulses to do oneself harm. Prompt, professional attention is indicated if one or more of these symptoms appears.

Some common coping behaviors can reach addictive proportions, becoming major problems in and of themselves by interfering in our relationship life or our work behavior and blocking any opportunity to move forward with our growth process. These include exercising, working long hours, overeating, and, most dangerously, alcohol or other drug use. When considering whether a relationship with chemicals or certain behaviors or activities have become unhealthy dependencies or addictive in nature, I often pay attention to several basic criteria: *mental obsession* (Do I spend a lot of time thinking about seeking, engaging in, or attempting to control the behavior or relationship with a substance?); *behavioral compulsion* (Do I engage in the behavior or activity when I consciously try not to? Do I engage excessively when I attempt to keep the behavior or activity in moderation?); *continuing despite consequences* (Do I continue with the behavior, activity, or relationship with substances despite negative consequences, such as work problems or job loss, health problems, legal repercussions, or concerns of friends and family?); *denial and shame dynamics* (Have I started to deny that I have a problem, despite the clear concerns of others? Have my failed attempts to manage or control left me with strong feelings of shame?); and, *a tendency toward relapse* (Have I ''fallen back'' into the old activity or relationship after a period of abstaining?). If the answer is ''yes'' to several of these questions (or even to just one or two of these questions), then professional attention or involvement in a 12 Step recovery program (for instance, Alcoholics Anonymous or Overeaters Anonymous), or both, may be indicated

A Few More Thoughts on Asking for Help

We all have been raised in a society, and many of us have been raised in a family, where asking for help and admitting pain and problems were deemed ''unmanly'', a sign of fundamental defectiveness. Whether we want to just understand ourselves better and improve our relationships with others, or whether we have started having other difficulties, such as stubborn depression or a developing chemical addiction, our defensiveness and our potential for deep shame tends to run high. Grieving our past, facing our painful present, and moving on to a more intimate and conscious type of relationship with ourselves and others, requires that we redefine what it means to be a man. This new definition must include being able to ask for help, developing care in our relationships, and making our emotional and physical well-being a priority. At certain critical times in our lives, such as a divorce, we stand at a developmental crossroads. Such times offer us a priceless opportunity, not only to learn from and heal from the hurts of the past, but to move forward to a fuller, richer life. This movement forward is not only rewarding for us, but allows us to be more available to those we care most deeply about, particularly our children.

<u>Nine</u>

Unnecessary Losses: Our Children

*"In watching my children struggle with the hurts and discontinuities
that are the inevitable result of the irreconcilable differences
between their parents, I have learned what many men learn only after
divorce. There is nothing more precious than our children.
In the quiet hours of the night, when I add up the accomplishments of
my life In which I take justifiable pride-- a dozen books, thousands of
lectures and seminars, a farm built by hand, a prize here, an honor
there-- I know three that rank above all the others are named Lael,
Gifford, and Jessamyn."*

- Sam Keen, *Fire in the Belly*

In Chapter One of this book, we had to accept the fact that
parenting, even under the best of circumstances, involves loss.
The bittersweet paradox of parenting is that if we do our job well,
our children will eventually leave us and move on with their own
lives. A mixture of pride and grief is the constant companion of
the conscious parent, as each step forward our child takes is,
indeed, experienced as a step away. We have seen how this basic
dilemma of parenting is made more powerful and painful for men
in the case of divorce. Days apart become weeks. Simple "good
nights" become prized treasures. The smell, the touch, the sound
of our children, once taken for granted, are replaced by long,
empty pauses. This emotional dislocation, the deep pain of
relationship separation, as well as the ambiguous and ambivalent
nature of the divorce process itself, can result in an often unnecessary distancing from our children.

     We cannot overlook the fact that some divorced fathers
lack contact with their children due to an unworkable relationship
with a former spouse, legal impediments, or other factors outside
a father's capacity to influence. *However, the most important
message of this book is that, all too often, men lose a consistent,
caring relationship with their children due to their own difficulties in recognizing and grieving their losses, accepting a new*

reality, and believing in their critical importance to their children's well-being. Indeed, it is often the more highly attached and involved father who has the most difficulty maintaining a close, meaningful connection with his children during the critical first, few months following separation and divorce.

Using our Pain and Paying Attention

Divorce, the gross shift in identity, and the shame and guilt that can flow from it, can drive many of us toward coping styles that temporarily dull our pain and confusion, but ultimately leave us alienated from ourselves and others. We must learn to use our pain as a sign that we need to pay attention. We need to pay attention to grieving our past losses and confusions in the families in which we grew up or formed on our own, and begin to see how past losses and separations impact the present. We need to pay attention to how our pain may have moved us toward a defensively exaggerated or distorted mode of maleness and then work toward a whole, authentic male emotionality and style of relatedness. We need to pay attention to how we may have developed compulsive or addictive coping behaviors to avoid our pain and confusion, begin to let go of these dysfunctional styles, and risk the pain and discomfort that inevitably accompanies growth. We need to pay attention to how we view the importance of fathers and acknowledge the effect that father-absence may have had in our own lives. Finally, we must affirm the critical importance of fathers in our own children's lives.

Getting Clear

Surprisingly, even after much time has passed, many men are not clear about what their divorce means in larger terms. What divorce means is that *our marriage is over but that our relationship with our children, while changed, continues.* These parts of our lives, our marriages and our relationships with our children, have been inextricably paired since before our children's births. They have been paired even before our children's conception, as we shared the hope, passion, and commitment of planning a family. Even the idea of parenting children outside of the marital context may seem foreign to us. The grief and confusion of separating out our role as fathers to our children from the sense of "normalcy" of children within a marriage, can be confusing. At one moment we may feel like we need to be back in our marriage to be with our children; the very next moment we may feel like we may need to give up our relationships with our children in order to end our marriage. In the end, we must do the difficult work of getting clear in our own heads and hearts that our marriage is over, but our relationship with our children continues.

Redefining and Affirming our Capacity to Nurture

The traditional concept of nurturing children brings forth visions of feeding, burping, diapering, comforting, and bathing. Indeed, men can and do perform these nurturing activities, with breastfeeding being the obvious exception to this rule. Unfortunately, following divorce, we may see ourselves as the "second" or less important parent, crippling our effectiveness as parents and minimizing the special nurturing that fathers may offer their children. We lose sight of what common sense and our own experience tells us, and what social science research confirms: *fathers are critically important to the healthy development of our children, whether they be male or female, younger or older.*

If we define nurturing as any activity that promotes the growth and development of our children, we see more clearly that fathers may provide a critically important type of nurturing that they may otherwise not receive. We may be our young children's first playmates, and gently draw their attention to the larger world outside of mother and the home. We may offer ourselves as another adult with whom to identify and as another source of validation of our children's specialness and loveability. As fathers, we may take responsibility for socializing our children by teaching them to play games, express their emotions, refrain from violence, win with humility, and lose with acceptance. We may offer a critically important perspective when making decisions about our children's education or the form of their religious observance. We may set limits and provide discipline. We may be our children's most important link to the larger world outside of home and school. Importantly, when we do perform the more traditional activities commonly considered to be nurturing, we offer our sons and daughters a model of flexible parenting, not tied to rigid sex role stereotypes.

Now, More than Ever

Yet another paradox of divorce is that at the very time that our children need us most, we may be unavailable to them. There are many aspects of parental divorce which, no doubt, have long-term effects on our children. One of the greatest hurts to children is the loss of their sturdy, consistent, predictable sense of home and family. Our own difficulties in working through a divorce, such as pulling away from our children out of shame, guilt, or rage, or our failure to come to terms with our past as it impacts the present, or our ambivalence and lack of confidence as parents, all these issues may complicate and compound the pain of the divorce experience for our children. *These, then, are the issues we must be committed to working through if we are to be emotionally available to them.*

Our children also require clear information from us, delivered in an understandable way. It is critically important not to assign blame to your spouse and, if it is true, to let our children know that both parents made attempts to improve the marriage. Most important, it is necessary to make it very clear to our children that they are in no way responsible for what happened and that both of their parents will continue to love them. In order to help our children not to experience divided loyalties, we must assure them that they are free to love both their parents. Since many children have fears for their safety and protection at the time of marital separation and divorce, it must be made clear that they will be well taken care of and not abandoned. As much as possible, give them basic details about what they can expect in their lives in the future, including where they will live, any changes in school, or custody. There is a limit, however, to how much and what type of information is appropriate for a child. Remarks must be tailored to the age and maturity level of your child. Encourage questions on an ongoing basis. Do not project your need to come to a sense of closure on your marital relationship onto your child. Children process information differently than adults do and may have a need to ask questions and gather more information as he or she grows older. For instance, a grade school child may have a new set of question about the divorce, from a much more sophisticated point of view, several years later when she is in high school.

Building a Home

The fact of the matter is that men most frequently end up leaving the family home at a time of relationship separation or divorce. Many men seem to make a particularly poor choice of a living situation when they separate and divorce. Frequently, men move in with a buddy and sleep on the living room couch or live in a low-rent, unfurnished apartment in a section of town miles away from their home and their children's school. *While there are often real financial constraints, many times these choices stem more from deep guilt, shame, and an impoverished sense of healthy entitlement, than from real financial circumstances.* Reflecting our internal pain, such choices may serve for us the neurotic purpose of punishing us for our failure to "provide and protect" or for some real failure or hurt we may have knowingly or unknowingly inflicted on our families. Yet, in the final analysis, remaining in such a setting only serves to keep us "stuck", depriving us and our children of a decent, comfortable home, and sets us up to long for home and family for, perhaps, exactly the wrong reasons.

> *Gene, a successful attorney, experienced deep pain and confusion at the time he and his wife made a joint decision for him to move out of the family home. "I'm going to sleep on a mattress on the floor, with the roaches picking at me," said Gene. While his initial choice of a place to live was not quite that difficult, it did lack adequate furniture, effective heating and cooling, and any sense that this was Gene's home, albeit a temporary one.*

> *As time passed, Gene found himself longing for an opportunity to return home, to lie on his comfortable couch, to flip through the channels on his big-screen television, to experience the comings and goings of his three young children. Notably lacking in Gene's*

*longings was much thought or feeling of returning to his
relationship with his wife. It was only after several
months of counseling and painful soul-searching that
Gene was able to allow himself a comfortable apartment, with separate bedrooms for his children, comfortably furnished, with objects and mementoes that reflected that this was both his and his children's home.*

We need a reasonably comfortable home, with familiar
pictures and comfortable furniture, or our record collection, or
our library. Similarly, our children, often emotionally dislocated
by the divorce, need to have a place with their dad, preferably with
their own bed, familiar toys, and pictures. Children (and adults
for that matter), need what psychologists call "transitional
objects": special toys, a familiar cereal bowl, a treasured
photograph, a favorite blanket, a football, or a doll set, to help
them feel connected to their source of security, their other more
established and secure home. For some children, this is a blanket,
a pillow, or a stuffed animal that goes back and forth between
Dad's and Mom's houses. Children also benefit from seeing Dad
living in a comfortable and pleasant manner, surrounded by
objects and mementoes which reflect a sense of "home." This
helps our children preserve a sense that both of their parents are
doing well and will continue to be available to them, and tends to
forestall a guilt-inducing sense that one of their parents is being
"victimized" by the other.

"Good Daddy"/"Bad Daddy"

At the time of relationship separation and divorce, and for
some time thereafter, we may be given to occasional swings of
guilt and shame, and an erosion of confidence in our competence
as a parent. At such times, we may be overly permissive or
indulgent toward our children. While this may give us short-term
satisfaction ("good daddy") and may temporarily assuage our
pain, this will eventually undermine our children's sense of
responsibility, their self-esteem, and, paradoxically, may leave
them feeling less protected in a world without firm limits and
expectations. Sometimes we may behave in an opposite manner,
striking out in an authoritarian mode, due to frustration, fatigue,
or confusion. Again, while this may be a short-term route to

structure and control, it leaves our children without the opportunity to develop decision-making skills, robs them of the opportunity to learn from the consequences of their behavior, and also undermines the development of self-esteem. Since we often tend to feel guilty over our extremely strict approach ("bad daddy"), we may swing back to the permissive mode, leaving our children without consistency and predictability at a time when they need these qualities to be present. All of us, especially under the stress of separation and divorce, coping with a new and more demanding parenting role, will be overly permissive, authoritarian, or swing from one style to the other, at times.

What is best for our children, and for us, is to work toward an *authoritative* approach to parenting. In this approach, we offer children choices and consequences. For instance, if their room is messy, they may be given a choice of cleaning up their room and watching a half hour of television before bedtime, or, alternatively, not cleaning up their room and forfeiting their TV time (or some other pleasurable activity). This allows the child to make decisions and to see a relationship between his or her behavior and the consequences. It offers the structure necessary to afford a sense of predictability and stability, and helps the child to see that they can make choices and have an impact on their world. The two keys to making this authoritative approach work are *consistency* and *choosing appropriate consequences* that are in keeping with the situation. For example, grounding a child for a month for not putting his or her dishes in the sink after dinner would be a consequence out of keeping with the demands of the situation.

Dad at Work

We have seen how our relationship with work can become distorted, a compulsive attempt to hide from our pain. Most often, however, fathers must work to support themselves and their children. For most of us, our work is a way we care for and nurture our children, as well as a way of creative expression and healthy productivity. At the time of divorce, financial demands may be greater than usual. We may find ourselves feeling guilty for the amount of time and energy we put into our jobs. However, provided that our relationship with work remains essentially healthy, we must allow ourselves to see our work as a supportive, nurturing activity in regard to our children. In other words, it is time to stop apologizing for working. To the extent that we are guilty and ashamed of our time and effort at work, we are less likely to invite our children into our world. This deprives them of the opportunity to see the world through our eyes and of being able to feel connected to us while we are away

Techniques for Staying Connected

Golant and Golant, in their fine book *Finding Time for Fathering*, mention a number of things we can do to maintain a sense of connection to our children, despite the fact that we may be working or may be separated from them. I have borrowed some items mentioned in their book and added some items of my own in the following list of concrete things we can do to maintain connection with our children, even in our absence·

1. Send cards and letters,
2. Use a ''transitional object'', something for your child to keep with him or her or put up in their room as a reminder of your involvement and affection,
3. Audio tape stories and letters,
4. Video tape a favorite show and watch it together with your child at a later time,
5. Agree to watch a TV show while apart and discuss it by phone later,
6. Buy your child a subscription to a magazine on a topic of interest to both of you and have the subscription delivered to your former spouse's address (if she agrees),
7. Make yourself available for help with homework by phone,
8. Use your telephone answering machine creatively, leaving personalized messages for your children,
9. Begin a crossword puzzle or chess game with your older child, and allow them to work on it on their own. Have him or her bring it back to you the next time they are scheduled to see you,
10. If both you and your children have access to a fax machine, use it as a way of communicating notes, homework, or articles of interest, and
11. Share information about your work with your chil-

dren in order to give them a vision of who you are and what you do while you are away from them.

"But It's Not Fair!"

Anyone who has gone through a divorce process, or, more importantly, has taken a hard look at their own life experiences, must know that life *is not* fair. Equality of time between parents is of some importance, but has not been shown to be of absolute importance. Within reason, the good that you do your child by being flexible, by not quibbling over minor aspects of a custody arrangement, by maximizing the time that you do have with him and her, and minimizing the pain of the time that you don't have with your child, greatly outweighs any efforts at technical equality. Certainly, if there is some gross inequity in a coparenting arrangement, a lack of fairness in the arrangement that impacts either parent's relationship with their child, this may need to be brought up to a spouse, often with the assistance of a counselor or mediator. What makes a child's relationship with both his or her parents positive and healthy depends less on the specific nature of a divorce and custody arrangement and more on the nature of the continuing relationship that exists between the parents. So much depends on the nature of our relationship with our children's mother, our former spouse.

Ten

Distant Dancing: Coparenting

*"It's been hard, working out this coparenting thing.
It's been hard for both of us. I sometimes have the thought that if
we can do this, why couldn't we make our marriage work. I think
that a lot when Derek gets ready to leave my house and go back to
his mom's. But I know in my heart that's not going to happen and
that my relationship with Derek is really a strong one. Maybe, in
some ways, it's even stronger than it could have been if his mom and
I had stayed married, With all the fighting, bad feelings. Too much
of my relationship with Derek got lost in our bad marriage; so maybe
there's a trade-off there.*

*- Denny, 32, reflecting on his coparenting of his 8 year old
son, Derek, almost two years after the end of his marriage.*

In the best of circumstances, both fathers and mothers
maintain a meaningful, consistent connection with their children
following divorce. Yet, despite the fact that the favorability of this
outcome is supported both by the force of common sense and
social science research, functional shared parenting seems to
occur all too infrequently. No doubt, the development of a
workable coparenting relationship is one of the most difficult
tasks facing us following divorce.

Getting Things Straight; Keeping Things Straight

In the last chapter, we examined how difficult it can be to
separate our relationship and emotional connection with our
former spouse from our bond with our children. Coparenting
may test this tenuous separation on an ongoing basis. Normal life
cycle events, such as birthdays and graduations, as well as
unexpected, emergent happenings such as illness or hospitaliza-
tions, may draw us back into a matrix of warm, caring, poignant
feelings about our child that are shared in intensity, perhaps, only
by our spouse. Indeed, in divorce situations where both partners

have worked through feelings about the split and have developed healthy (that is, firm but flexible) boundaries with the other, such feelings can be enjoyed or shared without threatening the integrity of the divorce and the primacy of the relationship with the child. Often, however, these feelings can be very confusing, leaving us in a quandary over what our feelings are and whom they are about. This is especially so early in a separation or divorce process.

The Pull Back; The Push Away

It is most common, even normal, for us to experience tugs, sometimes powerful tugs, back to a former spouse. Especially at times which evoke warm, poignant feelings, we may engage in a type of euphoric recall, remembering the happy, connected times with our former spouse. She may have a similar, reciprocal emotional experience. In such an atmosphere, the potential for regressive acting out of these feelings, sometimes in a sexual manner, is quite high.

>*Spence, a bright, attractive, witty financial planner, began therapy shortly after an unexpected, somewhat disturbing ''reunion'' with his former wife, Ann. Spence reported that after sharing the responsibility of organizing a party celebrating the 5th birthday of their daughter, Melissa, at Ann's home, Ann offered Spence a glass of wine if he would hang around and help clean up. In Spence's words, ''One thing led to another, and before I knew it I was staying for dinner. Then I stayed a bit longer to watch TV and then to put Melissa to bed. Well, uhm, I spent the night. And when Melissa woke up in the morning, she was very excited to see me and asked if I was moving back home. She was so upset when I said that I wasn't. I don't know what happened. It just felt so right and so good until the next day.''*

While there is no hard and fast rule prohibiting such reconnection, nor it is beyond possibility that such a reconnection could be the beginning of a healthy reconciliation, obviously the emotional risks are quite high. Most frequently, we are quickly reminded of why the relationship failed as a marriage in the first place. And we are often left with a bitter recycling through old, unresolved issues. Perhaps most hurtful is the likelihood that this reconnection, ignited during a time of emotional sharing around our children, winds up exposing them to yet another round of confusing behavior by their parents. This can be particularly damaging to the many children who maintain a reunion fantasy regarding their parents and who tenaciously cling to the idea that they, somehow, have a measure of responsibility or influence in bringing about such a reunion. In the end, we must accept a basic fact of healthy emotional development-- in order to be close in a healthy way, we must be able to be able to be comfortably separate and not prone to acting out our unresolved feelings and relationship issues.

Also common is the pushing away of our children because we experience confusion or upset regarding the divorce or our relationship with a former spouse when we are with our children. While fully understandable, such a generalized pain-avoidance strategy winds up compounding our pain by leaving us isolated from our children. They are then left with the additional loss of intimate contact with their father at a time when they are already experiencing significant loss and desperately need their relationships with adults to be predictable and sturdy. In this case, *we are faced with the central dilemma of keeping close to our children despite our pain, of grieving the loss of a marriage while still embracing the challenge of fatherhood.*

Pulling Out of the Blame-Shame Game

No matter how hard we work on the issue of shame and guilt over relationship loss and divorce, our failure to maintain the stereotyped idea of provider/protector may leave us vulnerable to occasional bouts of shame and guilt. Our former spouse may harbor similar deep feelings of guilt and shame, perhaps for somewhat different reasons than we do. Just as there are socially prescribed roles and duties unfairly projected upon men, women often internalize equally dysfunctional role expectations, such as the idea that they are supposed to "keep" a man in a marriage. Two people, carrying a significant measure of guilt and shame, will, under stress, feel a need to defend themselves with anger or by projecting their negative valuations of self onto the other person. The long-term solution requires each parenting partner to understand and work through their carried shame and their guilt after developing an atmosphere of boundaried respect with the other. Perhaps our best short-term strategy is to remind ourselves of the emotional stress of the coparenting situation, and to consciously develop a sense of emotional distance from our former spouse. We both need to maintain a strong focus on the importance of the task at hand, working together for the good of our children. Especially early in the divorce recovery process, our protective emotional boundaries are easily "unzipped." We must consciously guard against taking on shaming valuations of ourselves, while simultaneously not regressing into shaming and blaming our former spouse.

But We Parent Differently!

If we were fortunate enough to grow up in a relatively functional family, with two physically present and emotionally available parents, we will remember that Mom and Dad probably each had different ways of communicating with us, of disciplining us, of helping us with homework, or of playing with us. These differences may have been significant strengths, one complementing the other by offering us more than one parenting style and modeling for us an additional mode of coping with a complicated world. As marital relationships begin to have difficulty, as communication and emotional connection begin to come apart, differences tend to be viewed as bad or pathological. The tendency toward order and structure that once was prized by the other spouse is now seen as emotional sterility and a tendency towards being controlling. The emotional richness and spontaneity that once was so attractive in one's spouse is now seen by the other as immaturity and impulsivity. More often than not, relationships that result in separation and divorce have usually cycled through a painful period of identifying "intolerable" differences in the other spouse.

Sometimes, it seems like the capacity to appreciate and respect the other's differences is irretrievably lost. This dynamic may carry over to the coparenting relationship, with differences in personality, parenting style, and communication unnecessarily criticized in service of old, unresolved battles left over from the marriage Sadly, this leaves children in the untenable position of feeling like they must choose sides, or keep secrets, or "take care" of one parent by protecting the parent from the criticism or wrath of the other. This is not to say that gross differences in style of discipline, differences in bedtime, differences in expectations regarding homework, or, in the case of older children, differences regarding curfew or dating behavior, are positive. However, such gross, glaring differences also tend to stem from an inability to leave the pain and conflict of the marital relationship behind and work together cooperatively for the good of a child.

Communicating With the Former Spouse

Differences between former spouses become problems primarily when we fail to communicate adequately on issues related to parenting, leaving a large opportunity for one spouse to project his or her worst fears and expectations onto the other. This, of course, is the same dynamic that often occurs in troubled marriages. As difficult or as unlikely as it may seem, successful coparenting *requires* consistent communication, a reasonable level of respect for the other person's need for information and predictability, and a capacity to stay focused on the parenting task while not getting drawn into other emotional issues.

Early in the separation process, or when the wounds of divorce are still fresh, face-to-face communication, or even telephone contact, may be difficult. While such a defensive position cannot remain in place indefinitely, the temporary use of indirect communication techniques may allow some comfort during painful, emotionally raw periods. Telephone answering machines or fax machines can be successfully used to pass information regarding coparenting back and forth. Younger children, who carry backpacks to and from school, or between Mom's and Dad's house, may be given a special communication envelope labeled "For Parents Only." In any case, *do not* use your child as a conduit of information between you and your former spouse, particularly early in the separation or divorce process or during times of tension or conflict. The challenges that a child faces at such a time are great enough without adding the extra burden of being a "go-between" linking his or her parents. If a third person is necessary to ease communication for a period of time, choose an adult who seems reasonably objective and is not likely to get drawn into unhealthy dynamics.

Ultimately, however, regular face-to-face or phone contact is desirable in bringing about a healthy coparenting relationship that can address a full range of issues, from schedules to school work, from sports activities to medical concerns. Eventually, the coparenting relationship and the child are served by having occasional less structured "How's our kid doing?" conversations. Difficulties in moving towards this type of relatively open communication may be a sign of being "stuck" and also can present very real disadvantages, or even danger, to a child. Consulting a therapist experienced in divorce, communication, and coparenting issues can be most helpful in such a case

The Structure of Coparenting

My bias regarding parenting after divorce is clear. If at all possible, children seem to do best with substantial, consistent contact with both parents. Often, this end is attempted by arranging shared or dual custody, where both parents have legal custodial rights and a significant amount of time with their children. All too often, issues of fairness to a parent are raised, overlooking the emotional and developmental needs of the child. Even in the case of joint legal custody, the primary residence may best remain with one parent, particularly for the much younger child. At other times, depending on the needs of the child and the availability of both parents, more of an even split may be desirable. In rare instances, parents, in an effort to minimize the disruption of divorce, will agree to leave their children in one home and absorb the stress of moving from one residence to the other by making such moves themselves

Most frequently, fathers find themselves as the parent without primary custody and with limited visitation of their children. This predicament can be both painful and unwieldy, with successive reunions and leavetakings requiring a great deal of emotional energy and pulling the scab off the original wound of the separation and divorce.

Perry, a successful minor league baseball
manager, came to my office at the end of his second full

*baseball season with very little contact with his chil-
dren. Perry told a sad tale of pulling further and
further away from his 10 year old daughter and 6 year
old son and burying the pain of his separation from his
children in long hours of work and the geographic
transience that is a part of professional athletics.*

*"I thought I was doing okay by my kids," said
Perry. "I would send them a card from some city, or
send my son a baseball cap, and maybe even call them
from some far away place. But as time went on, it
became harder and harder, and eventually I stopped
making contact. I can't continue this. This is not all
right with me. I guess I needed some distance to deal
with my pain, but that wasn't the solution. I want to
develop a real relationship with my kids."*

As we have seen, a father's pulling away from his
children is usually not out of too little caring, but out of an inability
to deal with pain, out of a sense of being the "second", dispens-
able parent, and often out of a lingering sense of shame over the
divorce. It is precisely working through these issues and coming
to some level of resolution that makes coparenting work. *Even a
"part-time" father can be an extremely important, influential,
and emotionally connected father if he is able to work through
his own emotional issues, maintain a working relationship with
his former spouse, and be creative and flexible in maintaining
the bond with his children.*

Writing it Down

It is a fact in relationships that *healthy flexibility can only
develop from a position of structure.* Therefore, my strong
suggestion is that men work out a detailed and comprehensive
coparenting agreement with their former spouse. To some, this
seems unnecessary, even if the marital relationship had been a
difficult and contentious one. Of course, the goal of a flexible,
give-and-take relationship with a former spouse is a most worthy
one. Often, however, this is a fantasy, especially early during the
separation period and shortly after a divorce. It is for this reason
that a shared parenting agreement which spells out such issues as

weekly schedules, holiday schedules, vacations, shared expenses, and religious training must be developed. I have found that even the most well-intentioned parents often fall into deep upset and conflict over such issues as children's birthdays, important holidays, and vacation planning. Of course, flexibility within structure is beneficial not only for children, but for parents as well. But this flexibility must be supported by the building blocks of a clear coparenting agreement.

Communication and mutual respect become more and more important as our children grow older and as their needs change. Our parenting styles must also change to meet their developing needs. However, our children's needs are not the only things that change during a coparenting relationship. Sooner or later, one or both divorced parents may move on to a new relationship, stirring up feelings we may have believed were being comfortably managed.

<u>Eleven</u>

"Daddy's Got a Girlfriend": New Attachments

"Talk about guilt. Talk about just plain, old fear. Just the thought of risking another relationship makes me feel a bit crazy. And Cassie is pretty wary of Susan. On one hand, she really seems to like her; on the other, I think she feels guilty towards her mom when she does. The one thing I have worked hard at, though, is letting Cassie know she's not going to lose me if I see Susan."

- Burt, a 32 year old high school math teacher, divorced for 4 years, *discussing his developing relationship with his girlfriend, Susan, and his concerns of how it may affect his 12 year old daughter, Cassie.*

Sooner or later, a significant majority of divorced men decide to reenter new adult relationships and to remarry. A host of issues are raised by this decision, beginning with whether or not a new relationship is a healthy choice.

<u>Is Now the Time? Is This the Relationship?</u>

Some general guidelines may be considered regarding timing of new relationships. Obviously, an impulsive, passionate love affair during or shortly after a divorce is more likely to carry the seeds of emotional disaster than will a slowly nurtured, time-tested connection a few years following a divorce. However, we have already discussed how productive grieving and emotional growth are the products of much more than just time alone. Indeed, we have all known people whose emotional growth seems "stuck in time", people who seem to remain essentially emotionally unmoved by the losses and challenges of life. To be sure, we want to avoid the pain-driven immersion in a new marriage in an ultimately vain attempt to bind the wounds of relationship loss and reinstitute a sense of structure and support in our lives. Such a development is likely to be the premature propulsion to a new connection that we have already discussed in detail. As we have seen, our pain, our tendency to act out old, unresolved relationships and losses, must be dealt with directly and as consciously as possible. A simple rule-of-thumb is that *our relationships have a greater chance to be healthy if we enter them out of a sense of choice rather than out of deep need or compulsion.*

Entering relationships impulsively or out of need is unhealthy. Equally counterproductive is avoiding deeper relationships indefinitely out of a need for safety, or out of a hope that yet more reading, writing, therapy, or meditation may somehow "fix" us and do away with the intrinsic emotional risk of relationships. Here is what we owe to ourselves, and, indeed, to our children and those we might enter into a relationship with: 1) earnest and thoroughgoing efforts to grieve our losses, 2) understanding and working through our family of origin issues, 3) reclaiming our lost emotionality, 4) establishing emotionally supportive relationships with others (including other men), 5) developing consistent, caring relationships with our children, and 6) establishing a workable coparenting relationship with our former spouse. *These are the central, developmental tasks facing most men following divorce.* Beyond this, much of our further growth takes place within the context of a primary, adult relationship. It is here that we apply the benefits of our increased self-knowledge, our fuller emotionality, and our still developing capacity for intimacy.

Looking For Ms. Right

Just as the timing of a new relationship has less to do with months and years than it does with self-knowledge and emotional growth, *the health and success of a new relationship has as much to do with who we are in the relationship and the type of relationship we develop as it does with finding "the right partner."* We have only to look to the majority of ads in the personal section of the newspaper to see the tendency in our society to seek the "perfect" mate. While similarity of interests, background, and beliefs are of importance, searches for an ideal mate completely miss the point. Such an undertaking is bound to end in disappointment and disillusionment, for it is based on the literally childish wish for a "perfect" other to heal or complete the self. We must seek rather a more mature self-knowledge, and a realistic awareness of both the promise and limitations of relationships. Relationships based primarily on what the other can offer us are, by definition, not up to the messy, decidedly imperfect reality demands of relationships, in general. They are dangerously inadequate for the demands of relationships which involve divorced men and their children. Instead, we are generally best off in a relationship with a partner who, like us, has come to realize the value of self-knowledge and individual growth and recognizes the inherent difficulty of healthy relationships. Only when both partners come to realize that it is in relationships that we will continue our growth, and that this process is both rewarding and frustrating, will we truly be allies in one another's continued development.

What's Best for My Child?

Guilt is, of course, a familiar companion for most men who experience divorce. The separation and divorce experience is rife with situations and issues which leave us feeling like we have committed a tremendous wrong which we must try to right. Often, a measure of healthy guilt can move us toward increased introspection and positive behavioral change. Together with basic caring and concern, it may move us toward a more consistent, committed relationship with our children. However, guilt can become neurotic or unhealthy. It can pervade our thoughts and actions, leaving us forever feeling like we have done wrong and cannot give to ourselves and move forward with our own lives until we have atoned for our sins. It may leave us in an unhealthy position in relationship to our children, figuratively shackled to them and the task of caring for them. While this may serve to temporarily assuage us of our guilt, this is ultimately a very selfish position. All too often, a parent remains out of adult relationships due to their own fear or due to their own intimacy difficulties. This same parent may act as if it is their concern for his or her children that keeps them out of relationships. Our children, already burdened with the task of sorting out the responsibility for the failure of their parents' marriage, can wind up feeling terribly guilty themselves if a parent is unable to move on with his or her own life.

> *Brad and Cindy came to see me after almost two years of dating. The presenting complaint was that they were "unable to make a commitment and decide to get married." After some exploration, it turned out that Brad and Cindy began dating while Brad was still married to his former spouse. Brad very much felt that he was fully responsible for the breakup of his marriage. Cindy, whose own parents divorced when she was 8 years old, reexperienced her own early pain as a result of her relationship with Brad. Brad, who had shared custody of his five year old daughter, Abby, usually kept his schedule clear when his daughter was with him. The days that Abby was with Brad were full of individual attention for this little girl. For her part, Cindy found herself emotionally unable to spend any time with Brad when Abby was with him, even if Brad had invited such involvement.*
>
> *It was only after several months of therapy, both individually and together with Cindy, that Brad was able to understand the reasons for his largely exclusive relationship with his daughter, the potential burden this could place on this young girl, and the tremendous amount of guilt that both he and Cindy were carrying into their relationship.*

A particular paradox of divorced parents' relationships with their children is that developing new adult relationships can be beneficial to children. No child benefits, in the long run, from the burden of being his or her parent's sole object of love and attention. Certainly, one's own personal growth and the development of a secure, predictable relationship between father and child is necessary before considering a new adult love relationship. Indeed, such a relationship must have a reasonable degree of stability before a child is exposed or involved in the relationship. If possible, discussing the existence of the new relationship with the former spouse before involving the child is desirable in that it relieves the youngster of a "go-between" role and, perhaps, may even lessen the guilt toward his or her mother. Children, particularly girls, may feel a sense of rivalry with the "new woman" in Dad's life, as well as alternating feelings of like for her and guilt toward her own mother. However, in the end, children benefit if their father moves on to a new, stable adult love relationship. This removes them from a position of too much assumed responsibility for Dad's happiness and provides them a model of a relatively functional adult relationship which includes another grownup who cares for them.

If *She* Moves On

Statistically, men are more likely to remarry following a divorce; but the odds are still quite high that a former spouse will enter new relationship and, perhaps, remarry. Many a man, assumedly "past" his divorce, is taken aback by a curious mix of both relief and grief at a former spouse's new relationship. He may feel relief that she is continuing her life and has an opportunity for relationship happiness. He may feel grief at having to give up the final, irrational remaining fiction that she, somehow, might still be available to him (even if he has no realistic interest in actually returning to the old relationship). A former spouse's remarriage can, indeed, move us along to another emotional position. We may feel more alone, and our changed reality may jar us. If we have not remarried, we may reexperience feelings of being left. We may even enter a period of trying to "catch up" with our spouse and quickly make a new relationship connection for ourselves. If we have worked hard to learn more about ourselves, however, we may be conscious enough and trusting enough of our own unfolding growth process to know that what we are doing, even now, is yet a bit more grieving.

Coming Full Circle

We have now moved full circle-- from the early, stinging pain of marital separation, through our own period of self-examination and growth, to the development of caring, connected relationships with our children following divorce, to the establishment of new, adult love relationships. Throughout this process, we have been struggling to know ourselves better and to be available emotionally to our children and others that we love and care about. One constant, one undeniable truth, has continued to make itself known throughout our journey. *Life is a dance of connecting and letting go, of rejoicing and grieving, of loss and renewal, and, then again, of loss.* The paradox of acknowledging this poignantly painful, fundamental fact is that it allows us to not shrink away from the sorrow of life and, thereby, to more fully embrace the passion and purpose of our existence.

<u>Epilogue</u>

Morning mist rose from the glistening mountain meadows as the low-lying sun cast long shadows across the road ahead. My daughter and I rolled along the endless highway toward Salt Lake City. This was to be the first time she visited her birthplace since she was four months old. The trip was an opportunity for my daughter to see the first house that sheltered her. It was an opportunity for her to visit the hospital in which she was delivered eight years earlier. It was an opportunity for her and for me, alone and uninterrupted, to discuss her parents' marriage and divorce. As hours and miles passed, her questions poured forth in an uneven flow. She had tried to solve this puzzle before, but this time her queries carried with them a new level of insight. I could sense my daughter's quick mind, hidden behind dark brown eyes, register fresh information and make new connections. A curious mixture of pain and relief came over me as I realized that our conversation, as difficult as it was at times, offered both of us a chance for more healing.

It was during a pause in our talk, when we were both reflecting on what had been said, that two young, antlered deer burst across the highway. I slowed the car to avoid hitting them. I slowed it further so we could watch their regal romp into the safety of the thick, green brush. In a moment, they were gone. Both my daughter and I laughed with glee at our proximity to this simple wonder of nature. I sensed that our trip was somehow blessed by the sudden appearance of the deer that morning, much the same way that my life's journey had been so deeply enriched by my relationship with the little girl sitting beside me.

Over two years have passed since that trip. The quality and meaning of my life has been enhanced by the development of a loving relationship with a new partner, as well as by the addition of two remarkable and challenging children. My first daughter has yet another caring adult in her life, and a brother and sister with whom to play and argue. She is less the little girl now, as a larger world beckons to her daily. Every step forward is, indeed, a step away. The task of being an emotionally connected father, the bittersweet struggle of holding her close and letting her go, has left me both immeasurably rewarded and, on occasion, significantly saddened. I would not have my life any other way.

References

Introduction:
Averill, J.R. and Nunley, E.P. (1988). Grief as an emotion
    and as a disease: A social-constructionist perspective.
    Journal of Social Issues, 44(3), 79-96.
Berman, C. (1991). *A hole in my heart: Adult children of
    divorce speak out*. New York: Simon & Schuster.
Medved, D. (1989). *The case against divorce*. New York:
    Ballantine Books.
Peck, J.S. and Manocherian, J.R. (1989). Divorce in the
    changing family life cycle. *In* B. Carter and M.
    McGoldrick (eds.), *The changing family life cycle. A
    framework for family therapy*. Boston, MA: Allyn
    and Bacon .
Wallerstein, J.S. and Blakeslee, S. (1989). *Second chances:
    Men, women, and children a decade after divorce*.
    New York: Ticknor and Fields.

Chapter One:
Viorst, J. (1987). *Necessary Losses*. New York: Ballantine
Books.

Chapter Two:
Ainsworth, M.D.S. and Bowlby, J. (1991). An ethological
    approach to personality development. *American
    Psychologist, 46*, 333-341.
Bowlby, J. (1982). *Attachment and loss: Vol. 1 Attachment*
    (2nd ed.). New York: Basic Books.
Heard, D. (1978). From object relations to attachment theory:
    A basis for family therapy. *British Journal of Medical
    Psychology, 51*, 67-76.

Heard, D. (1982). Family systems and the attachment dy-
    namic. *Journal of Family Therapy, 4*, 99-116.
Kessler, S. (1975). *The American way of divorce: Prescrip-
    tions for change* Chicago: Nelson-Hall.
Klein, M. (1960). *Our adult world and its roots in infancy*.
    London: Tavistock Publications.
Kubler-Ross, E. (1969). *On death and dying*. New York:

MacMillan.

Lundin, T. (1984). Long-term outcome of bereavement. *British Journal of Psychiatry, 145*, 424-428.

Mahler, M., Pine, F., and Bergman, A. (1975). *The psychological birth of the human infant.* New York: Basic Books.

Parkes, C.M. (1972). *Bereavement: Studies of grief in life.* New York: International Universities Press.

Pine, F. (1989). The place of object loss in normal development. *In* David R. Dietrich and Peter C. Shabad (eds.) *The Problem of Loss and Mourning: Psychoanalytic Perspectives.* New York: International Universities Press.

Wolfelt, A. (1988). *Death and grief: A guide for clergy.* Muncie, Indiana: Accelerated Development.

Wortman, C.B. and Silver, R.C. (1989). The myths of coping. *Journal of Consulting and Clinical Psychology, 57*, 349-357.

Chapter Three:

Bradshaw, J. (1988). *Healing the shame that binds you.* Deerfield Beach, Florida: Health Communications, Inc.

Carnes, P. (1983). *Out of the shadows: Understanding sexual addiction.* Minneapolis, MN: CompCare.

Chan, C. (1987). Addicted to Exercise. *1987 Medical and Health Annual, Encyclopedia Britannica*, 429-432.

Fossum, M. and Mason, M. (1986). *Facing shame: Families in recovery.* New York: W.W. Norton & Company

Friel, J. and Friel, L. (1988). *Adult children: The secrets of dysfunctional families.* Deerfield Beach: Health Communications, Inc.

Kaufman, G. (1985). *Shame: The power of caring.* Cambridge, Mass: Schenkman Books, Inc.

Kets De Vries, M. (1989). Alexithymia in organizational life: The organization man revisited. *Human Relations, 42*, 1079-1093.

Kipnis, A. (1991). *Knights without armor: A practical guide for men in quest of masculine soul.* Los Angeles, CA:

Jeremy P. Tarcher, Inc.
Robinson, B. (1989). *Work addiction: Hidden legacies of
    adult children*. Deerfield Beach, Florida: Health
    Communications, Inc.
Staudacher, C. (1991). *Men and grief: A guide for men
    surviving the death of a loved one*. Oakland, CA:
    New Harbinger Publications, Inc.

Chapter Four:
Buehler, C. (1987). Initiator status and the divorce transition.
    Family Relations, 36, 86-90.
Fossum, M. and Mason, M. (1986). *Facing shame: Families
    in recovery*. New York: W.W. Worton & Company.
Hetherington, E.M. and Cox, R. (1981). Effects of divorce on
    parents and children. *In* M. Lamb (ed.),
    Nontraditonal families . Hillsdale, NJ: Erlbaum.
Myers, M.F. (1986). Angry, abandoned husbands: Assess-
    ment and treatment. *In* R.A. Lewis and M.B.
    Sussman (eds.). *Men's changing roles in the family*.
    New York: Haworth Press.

Chapter Five:
Ainsworth, M.D.S., Blehar, M.C., Waters, E., and Wall, S.
(1978). *Patterns of attachment: A psychological study of the
strange situation*. Hillsdale, NJ: Erlbaum.
Bowlby, J. (1982). *Attachment and loss: Vol 1 Attachment*.
    (2nd ed.). New York: Basic Books.
Kipnis, A. (1991). *Knights without armor: A practical guide
    for men in quest of masculine soul*. Los Angeles, CA:
    Jeremy P. Tarcher, Inc.
Satir, V. (1988). *The new peoplemaking*. Mt. View, CA:
    Science & Behavior Books.
Wegscheider, S. (1981). *Another chance: Hope and health
    for the alcoholic family*. Palo Alto, CA: Science &
    Behavior Books.

Chapter Six:

James, J.W. and Cherry, F. (1988). *The grief recovery
    handbook*. New York: Harper & Row.

Pollock, G.H. (1989). The mourning process, the creative
 process, and the creation. *In* David R. Dietrich and
 Peter C. Shabad (eds.) *The problem of loss and*
 mourning: Psychoanalytic perspectives. New York:
 International Universities Press.
Staudacher, C. (1991). *Men and grief: A guide for men*
 surviving the death of a loved one. Oakland, CA:
 New Harbinger Publications, Inc.

Chapter Seven:
Doutherty, P. (1990) A personal perspective on working with
 men in groups *In* D. Moore and F. Leafgren (Eds.)
 Problem solving strategies for men in conflict.
 Alexandria, VA: American Association for Counsel-
 ing and Development.
Kaufman, G. (1985). *Shame: The power of caring.* Cam-
 bridge, MA: Schenkman Books, Inc.
Kipnis, A. (1991). *Knights without armor: A practical guide*
 for men in quest of masculine soul. Los Angeles, CA:
 Jeremy P. Tarcher, Inc.
Kets De Vries, M. (1989). Alexithymia in organizational life:
 The organization man revisited. *Human Relations,*
 42, 1079-1093.

Chapter Eight:
Bowlby, J. (1988). Developmental psychiatry comes of age.
 American Journal of Psychiatry, 145, 1-10.
Donohue, W. (1991). *Communication, marital dispute, and*
 divorce mediation. Hillsdale, NJ: Lawrence Erlbaum
 Associates, Inc.
Freud, S. (1957). Mourning and melancholia. In *Standard*
 Edition of Complete Psychological Works of Sigmund
 Freud, (Vol. 14). London: Hogarth Press.
Kaufman, G. (1985). *Shame. The power of caring.* Cam-
 bridge, MA: Schenkman Books, Inc.
Kingma, D.R. (1993). *The men we never knew: Women's*
 role in the evolution of a gender. Berkeley, CA:
 Conari Press.
Sullivan, H.S. (1953). *Interpersonal theory of psychiatry.*
 New York: Norton.

Tannen, D. (1990). *You just don't understand: Women and men in conversation.* New York: Ballantine Books.
Wolfelt, A. (1988). *Death and grief: A guide for clergy.* Muncie, IN: Accelerated Development, Inc.

Chapter Nine:

Golant, M., & Golant, S. (1992). *Finding time for fathering.* New York: Ballantine Books.
Kruk, E. (1994). The disengaged custodial father: Implications for social work practice with the divorced family. *Social Work, 39,* 15-25
McKay, M., Rogers, P., Blades, J., & Gosse, R. (1984). *The divorce book.* Oakland, CA: New Harbinger Publications.

Chapter Ten:

Brown, F.M. (1989) The post-divorce family. *In* B. Carter & M. McGoldrick (eds.), *The changing family life cycle: A framework for family therapy* (2nd ed.) . Boston: Allen and Bacon.
Fossum, M. & Mason, M. (1986). *Facing shame: Families in recovery.* New York: W. W. Norton & Co.
Maccoby, E., & Mnookin, R. (1992). *Dividing the child: Social and legal dilemmas of custody.* Cambridge, MA: Harvard University Press.

Chapter 11:

Brown, F.H. (1989). The post divorce family. *In* Betty Carter and Monica McGoldrick (eds.) *The changing family life cycle: A framework for family therapy* (2nd ed.). Boston, MA: Allyn and Bacon.
Hendrix, H. (1988). *Getting the love you want: A guide for couples.* New York: Harper & Row.
Wallerstein, J.S. and Blakeslee, S. (1989). *Second chances: Men, women, and children a decade after divorce.* New York: Ticknor and Fields.

Barnes & Noble Bookseller
1800 Rosecrans Avenue, Building B
Manhattan Beach, CA 90266
(310) 725-7025
04-02-07 S02986 R005

CUSTOMER RECEIPT COPY

BARNES & NOBLE MEMBER   EXP:07-31-07

CUSTOMER ORDER PICKUP
ORDER NUMBER   2986-145132

Divorced Dad Dilemma   8.95
9780595141920
DISCOUNT   9.95 - 1.00
****

Circle: How the Power of   15.16
9781585421109
DISCOUNT   18.95 - 3.79
Vital Friends: The Peopl   18.36
9781595620071
DISCOUNT   22.95 - 4.59

SUB TOTAL   42.47
SALES TAX   3.50
TOTAL   45.97
AMOUNT TENDERED
MASTERCARD   45.97
CARD #:   ***********1368
AMOUNT   45.97
AUTH CODE   048684

MEMBER SAVINGS   9.38

TOTAL PAYMENT   45.97
         Thank you for Shopping at
         Barnes & Noble Booksellers
#437229 04-02-07 01:23P Pam

Printed in the United States
72942LV00002B/4